OUR GOD

Are you in doubt concerning Allah,
Maker of the heavens and the earth?
(The Holy Quran, 14:11)

Our God

(Hamārā Khudā)

Proving the existence of God by rational means

by

Ḥaḍrat Mirza Bashir Ahmad, M.A.

ISLAM INTERNATIONAL PUBLICATIONS LTD.

Our God

An English rendering of *Hamārā Khudā,*
written by Ḥaḍrat Mirza Bashir Ahmad[ra], M.A.

First Urdu edition published in Qadian, India, 1927
First English translation published in the UK, 2007
(ISBN 1-85372-878-0)
Present second revised edition published in the UK, 2016

Published by
Islam International Publications Ltd.
(Additional Wakālat-e-Taṣnīf)
Islamabad, Sheephatch Lane
Tilford, Surrey GU10 2AQ, UK

For further information please visit www.alislam.org.

ISBN-978-1-84880-861-4
10 9 8 7 6 5 4 3 2

CONTENTS

ABOUT THE AUTHOR

Ḥaḍrat Mirza Bashir Ahmad^ra was born to the Promised Messiah^as on 20 April 1893, according to the Divine prophecy: *Qamarul-Anbiyā'* [The Moon of the Prophets] will arrive and your affair will become manifest. Soon a son will be born to you and grace will come close to you.

He passed his matriculation with distinction in 1910 and received an M.A. in Arabic in 1916, in compliance with the wish of the Promised Messiah^as.

With the blessings of Allah, the prayers of the Promised Messiah^as, the guidance given to him by his elder brother, Ḥaḍrat Khalīfatul-Masīḥ II^ra, and his God-given abilities, he was able to serve the Ahmadiyya Muslim Jamā'at throughout his life in various capacities.

He was a great religious scholar, a prolific writer, and his books, articles, and speeches are easily comprehensible to an average reader. He wrote on numerous topics; his magnum opus is *Sīrat Khātamun-Nabiyyīn* [The Life and Character of the Seal of the Prophets]. *Sīratul-Mahdī, Silsilā-e-Aḥmadiyya,*

Tablīgh-e-Hidāyat, Kalimatul-Faṣl, and the present work,
Hamārā Khudā, are some of his important works.

Apart from his books, he contributed many articles, the number of which runs into hundreds, to the Jamā'at dailies and peri-
odicals, especially *Al-Fazl.*

He was a man of God, the recipient of Divine revelations
and visions and would not disclose them except rarely. One of
his revelations was *'Assalāmu 'alaikum'* [Peace be upon you] and
another was:

اٹھ محمدی تیری سربلندی کا وقت قریب آگیا ہے ۔

*That is, 'Rise Muhammadī, the time of your eminence has
drawn close'.*

He passed away on 2 September 1963, at the age of 71.

FOREWORD TO
THE 2007 EDITION

I have been asked to write a brief preface to the English translation of the book *Hamārā Khudā* [Our God], written in Urdu by
my father, Ḥaḍrat Mirza Bashir Ahmad, when he was in the prime
of his youth.

My deepest and abiding impression about my father centres
around his total submission and unbounded love for Allah, the
Holy Prophet[saw] of Islam, and the Promised Messiah[as]. It seemed
as if his whole life revolved around them. In family gatherings,
particularly when addressing his children, he would narrate some
story about each of his three loves and his eyes would be filled
with tears through intense emotions. In my mind, I can see him
now as if this happened only today, when in fact the incidents
relate to some seventy odd years ago. It is no surprise that this
should be so, because of the total sincerity and utter devotion
with which he addressed us.

It is therefore no coincidence that he wrote books on these

three topics which directed his life and consumed his attention. Apart from his book *Hamārā Khudā* [Our God], written largely for the youth who were being swept by the onslaught of atheist literature, after great research he also wrote a *Sīratun-Nabī*[1] in three volumes. This was received with great appreciation and jubilation, even among eminent non-Ahmadi personalities like Sir Muhammad Iqbal. What impressed the readers most was his convincing defence and clarification of topics which had attracted a great deal of criticism in the West, such as slavery, polygamy, the true concept of Jihad, wars of self-defence and total prohibition of pressure or use of force in matters of faith and conscience.

His other book in this category is the work related to *Sīrat-ul-Mahdī*,[2] again published in three volumes. It was also written with great love and devotion ensuring the chain of command through which the incidents in the Promised Messiah's[as] life were recorded.

Let me in the end make a humble request for prayers for my father. Please, whenever possible, offer a little prayer for him; his soul will rejoice and his children will remain eternally grateful.

M.M. Ahmad
Amīr
Ahmadiyya Muslim Community, USA
July 2002

---

1. Refers to the Urdu title, *Sīrat Khātamun-Nabiyyīn*, which has been translated into English under the title of *The Life and Character of the Seal of the Prophets* (2 vols.). [Publisher]

2. Life of the Mahdi[as] [Publisher]

FOREWORD TO
THE PRESENT EDITION

In the nineteenth and twentieth centuries, Western philosophers such as Friedrich Nietzsche (1844–1900), who coined the phrase 'God is dead', and Sigmund Freud (1856–1939), who postulated that God and religious teachings are illusions to accommodate for human psychological and social needs, led a nascent movement promoting atheist beliefs. When Christian clerics were unable to reconcile their beliefs regarding God in light of scientific discoveries, people began to fall away from belief altogether. Gradually, the misperception that science somehow contradicted religion became widespread, infecting members of every revealed religion, including Islam.

The Holy Founder of the Ahmadiyya Muslim Community, Ḥaḍrat Mirza Ghulam Ahmad[as] (1835–1908), taught that the laws of nature and the laws of religion emanate from the same Source—God—and can never be in contradiction. Thus, the *works* of God and the *words* of God are always in harmony with one another. Ḥaḍrat Mirza Ghulam Ahmad[as], the Promised Messiah and Imam Mahdi, championed Islam and the Holy Quran by proving their teachings to be both rational and miraculous, while harmonizing them with the principles of science.

In the same vein, Ḥaḍrat Mirza Bashir Ahmad[ra], M.A. (1893–1963), in his Urdu treatise *Hamārā Khudā,* masterfully explains that reason and science point to the existence of God. The author replies to the most common questions, doubts, and objections relating to God's existence. He explains why and how we should investigate the existence of God, enumerates the benefits of belief in God, and addresses several arguments atheists put forward to deny God. Although intended for youth, who are easily swayed by hollow arguments that erroneously invoke science and reason, the book has earned the appreciation of a much broader readership.

Our God is an English translation of *Hamārā Khudā.* Initial translations were prepared by Bilal Khalid and Dr. Munawar Ahmad, with assistance from Raja Ata-ul-Mannan, Zulkarnain, and Mirza Anas Ahmad, M.A., M.Litt., (Oxon.), Wakīlul-Ishāʿat, Rabwah, and his team, as well as Dr. Waseem Ahmad Sayed, who revised the present manuscript. Additionally, Abdul-Quddus Arif, Hassan Faiyaz Khan, Sardar Anees Ahmad, Syed Faraz Hussain, Salman Muhammad Sajid, Abdul-Wahab Mirza, and Naveed Ahmed Malik assisted in various capacities to prepare this book for publication. May Allah abundantly reward them for their efforts. *Āmīn.*

Munir-ud-Din Shams
Additional Wakīlut-Taṣnīf
London, May 2016

OUR GOD

$$\text{بِسْمِ اللهِ الرَّحْمٰنِ الرَّحِيْمِ} \ ^1$$
$$\text{نَحْمَدُهُ وَنُصَلِّى عَلٰى رَسُوْلِهِ الْكَرِيْمِ} \ ^2$$
خدا کے فضل اور رحم کے ساتھ۔ ھو الناصر ^{3}

INTRODUCTION

I have long wanted to write a book on the subject of the existence of God, for the benefit of young people in particular. I wanted to set out in a brief and simple manner the arguments which prove the existence of God—who is our Master and Creator—and to describe His attributes and the advantages and means of establishing communion with Him. For a number of reasons, I have, until now, been unable to fulfil this desire. A few days ago, however, someone[4] asked me about the existence of God in his own

---

1. In the name of Allah, the Gracious, the Merciful. [Publisher]

2. We praise Him, and invoke blessings on His Noble Messenger[saw]. [Publisher]

3. With the grace and mercy of Allah. He is the Helper. [Publisher]

4. This person has since passed away. May Allah the Exalted treat him with forgiveness, grace, and mercy.

peculiar manner, thus rekindling my old desire. I took this to be
an appeal from beyond and embarked upon writing this book.

وَمَا تَوْفِيقِيۤ اِلَّا بِاللّٰهِ ۚ عَلَيْهِ تَوَكَّلْتُ وَ اِلَيْهِ اُنِيْبُ¹

It would be incorrect to think that I have prepared myself for this
task, or that I wish to shed any light upon it from a purely intellectual point of view. The only purpose I have in mind is to share my
existing knowledge on the subject with the young and ordinary
people in a simple and concise manner. If God so wills, it might
grant guidance to some lost soul, or refresh someone's stagnating
faith, or serve to comfort some anxious and restless heart, or, perchance, our dearly beloved might come to realise that the true aim
and purpose of our lives is to recognise our Lord, whose love is
greater than any other.

Before I begin I pray to the Almighty: 'O my Lord, You
are aware of all my shortcomings and my knowledge and deeds
are not hidden from You. Grant me, through Your grace, the
strength to complete this book in accordance with that which
pleases You. Grant power to my words and lead my pen along the
path of righteousness and truth, so that people may recognise You
and attain the goal of their lives. O my Helper and Guide, though
I consider myself true in my intentions, You know me better than
I know myself. If You are aware of any ill-intentions on my part,
do have mercy on me and purify me so that this book may not be
deprived of the blessings which You send down in support of the

---

1. There is no power in me save through Allah. In Him do I trust and to
   Him do I return. (*Sūrah Hūd*, 11:89). [Publisher]

truth. Be it so, O my Lord and Master, O Thou who art the Most Merciful of those who show mercy, *Āmīn!*

The Plight of Faith in the Present Age

First of all, I want to express extreme regret at the belief in God held in common by some people in this age. On the face of it, all religions of the world believe in the existence of God. Their followers profess the same faith, except for an insignificant minority which openly denies His existence. But when we carefully examine the situation, we find that belief in God is based on form rather than substance. People have inherited this belief from their ancestors and feel obliged to adhere—albeit ostensibly—to the fundamentals of their religions. They do not want to abandon it lest society disintegrates, but in their heart of hearts they do feel that God may indeed exist. For these reasons they dare not deny His existence and believe that they have a God. But in reality they do not believe in God and their hearts are as devoid of faith as a deserted house is of inhabitants.

This is not only true of some particular country or religion; it is rather true of all religions and of the entire world. The poison of disbelief has penetrated deep into the followers of all religions: be they Zoroastrians, Buddhists, Hindus, Jews, Christians, Sikhs, or Muslims, etc. The searing and noxious winds of materialism have reduced every orchard of faith to ashes. If anyone seeks verity of this claim, I can adduce such evidence that cannot be denied by any fair-minded person. To those who doubt it, I will ask just one question: After analysing the state of their own hearts and of their fellows, can they honestly say that they all truly believe in God? I speak not of superficial or inherited ritual, but of true and living faith. Do they feel and experience the existence of God as they feel and experience the material and tangible things of this world? Are they as certain about the existence of God as they are about the existence of the sun, the moon, the mountains, the rivers, their houses, their ancestors, and their friends? If not, then understand it well that we cannot consider their faith to be true. They are not in the least certain about the existence of God, and can be likened to those who hold on to a rotten corpse imagining it to be alive.

If they say that the faith and conditions of faith I have mentioned above are of the highest possible level and that only the elect of God are blessed with such a lofty station, their statement would lend further proof of their ignorance, for they know nothing of the highest level of faith and can hardly begin to appreciate it. The fact is that this level of faith—whereby one believes in God just as one believes in material objects of this world—is only a middle level of faith. Have you not read the hadith in which the Holy Prophet^{saw} has said that a believer with the average level of faith would prefer to be burnt to ashes rather than abandon his creed? But if one finds himself at the lower level of faith, then let me ask: Can you honestly say that your faith influences your life as a living truth in reality? Do you really feel the love of God and the fear of His wrath in your heart? Does your faith induce you to do good and to discard evil? Do you truly put your trust in God, in all things, rather than in material means?

I do not mean to ask whether or not you sometimes feel any relationship with God, or whether thinking about Him prevents you from evil, because such a condition could be true even of a person who has insight enough not to deny the existence of God. Every now and then, the idea occurs to him that God, who has created him and controls the universe, may indeed exist and that some day he may have to be answerable to Him. Of course, such a person would feel a certain association with the idol of an imaginary god, and this thought may at times stop him from sin and urge him to do good, and he might at times manage to look beyond the material things towards God and feel that real trust can only be placed in Him. But such a state cannot be called true faith, rather it is a state of doubt which keeps him swaying like a pendulum. It can only be called true faith when it becomes a permanent part of one's life and takes root in one's heart as an eternal truth. It should become the food for his soul and a beacon to warn him of all the dark alleys of sin. Through such faith the paths of righteousness are illuminated for him and all material things lose their significance. He no longer depends on material means but places his real trust in God—the ultimate Cause of all causes. The fire of Divine love continues to blaze in his heart, and the fear of earning His displeasure overwhelms his entire being.

Do you really find such faith in your hearts? If not—and that is most likely to be the case—then please do not claim that you are believers. Seek instead true faith which descends from heaven and lights up the farthest and darkest recesses of the heart like a powerful lamp. When this happens, God shall cease to be a figment of your imaginations and shall reveal Himself in His true form, as a Living, Self-Subsisting and Omnipotent Sovereign, who is Loving and Kind. His Kingdom shall become far more evident and manifest than that of earthly monarchs.

True faith, in short, is conspicuous by its absence in the present age. Not only is it absent from the hearts of the masses, but those who profess to be the leaders of religion and claim to be custodians of people's faith have themselves fallen prey to atheism. They either deceive the world or are themselves deceived. Their lips profess but their hearts are empty. When it comes to spirituality, the world has indeed fallen into an abyss of darkness and there is not the tiniest flicker to guide a staggering and stumbling wayfarer. Is it not the demand of the age that in keeping with God's eternal practice, the Sun of His Manifestation should rise from the heart of a holy person and illuminate the world?

My dear people! Prostrate yourselves before the Divine threshold, for God has seen your plight and has raised a Spiritual Sun from the Eastern horizon. Open the windows of your hearts and let the pure rays of this Sun dispel the darkness of doubt and suspicions, so that the night of darkness may turn into a bright day!

If There is a God, Why Can We Not See Him?

I would first like to remove one misconception which commonly besets people with regard to the existence of God. If there is a God, why are we not able to see Him? This is hardly a new question, and we have heard it from time immemorial. The Holy Quran tells us that the same question was put to the Holy Prophet[saw] by the non-believers of Arabia.[1] Whenever I hear people raising this question, I feel sorry for them. It is such a pity that when man stumbles and his reason becomes blunted by the veils of indifference, he

---

1. *Sūrah Banī Isrāʾīl*, 17:93.

starts denying even self-evident truths. When this objection was raised in the past—however absurd and baseless it was—it had the potential to deceive some ignorant people. But what surprises me is that this objection should be raised in the present age! I am truly astonished at the intellect of people who use such objections to justify their denial of God. But as it is a common objection, I will proceed to answer it, albeit briefly.

There are different ways of learning about things. For instance, we learn by sight, sound, taste, smell, texture, or movement. All information we derive from the various senses, have the same degree of authenticity and credibility. We cannot demand that we must learn about something through a particular sense, or else we shall deny its very existence. The eyes, for example, are the medium for perceiving different colours; the nose is used for discerning different smells; and, the ears are for hearing sounds. Would it not be sheer insanity to insist that unless we could see a certain smell with our eyes, or smell a particular colour with our nose, or feel a particular sound with our hands, we shall not believe that it exists? Whoever makes such demands would be considered insane, and if perchance he is not sent to the lunatic asylum, he will certainly become a laughing stock for the street urchins. Strange to say, people raise such objections about God all the time and are still considered wise! Do they find nothing other than God to make the object of their mockery?

So far I have mentioned only the physical senses through which we acquire knowledge of various worldly phenomena. But there are countless other things which we cannot experience through any of our physical senses. Yet we have the same degree of certainty about them as about the others. Take the magnetic force, for instance. Can we see it with our eyes, or hear it with our ears, or smell it with our noses, or taste it with our tongues, or touch it with our hands? No, but none of us ever denies its existence. Despite not being able to perceive magnetic force through our common senses, we certainly do not refute its reality, because we can categorically observe the effects and impact of this force, and it creates the same degree of certainty as gained by direct perception. When we see an ordinary piece of iron being pulled by a magnet, and we see this happen every time, this leads us to conclude that there must be a force in the magnet. We do not see the force of magnetism, but we believe that the magnet has some additional force, besides its obvious properties, which can only be observed by its characteristics and not directly through our senses. Likewise, there is electricity, which is not visible, but commands our conviction because of its effects. With the flip of a switch, we can promptly make a fan in the room spin, confirming that the fan is driven by an external power that was there before we pressed the button. Although we cannot see, hear, smell, taste, or perceive it through any of the common senses directly, we are convinced that electricity is a great power. This is because we witness its effects and never for a moment deny its existence. We believe in it just as we believe in the sun, the moon, the mountains and the rivers.

Consider the sentiment of love. Has anyone ever seen, heard, smelled or touched love? If there is any reader of this book who truly cherishes love and has felt it in his heart, I ask him whether he has not experienced in his small heart—which might weigh less than half a pound—the boundless sea of love, which, can be considered one of the most powerful and awesome of natural forces in a storm. It generates so much energy and power into the feeble human frame, that for the sake of the beloved he challenges the mountains, roams the deserts, takes on the beasts of the jungle, jumps into fires and faces the raging tempests of the sea, but never gives up. He keeps vigil during the nights, wanders about during the day like one possessed and his life ebbs from his eyes, but never wearies. Is there anyone who can deny the existence of this force, even though no one has ever seen, heard, smelled, tasted or touched it? Time, age, power, sense, lust, anger, mercy—to mention but a few—are examples of things which we believe in but they have never been directly perceived by our physical senses.

It is, therefore, childish to insist that unless we obtain knowledge of something by a particular means, we will not believe in its existence. The point is to gain knowledge from whichever direction it comes. Once the purpose is attained all else is resolved.

If someone says that he will only believe that he has seen inside a room if he is led into it by breaking the roof and not if he simply enters through the door, I would suspect that he wishes to blow off the roof rather than see the room. Once he has entered the room, it matters not whether he entered through the roof or through the door. After all you can only enter through the passage specified for it. To demand a passage of one's own choice is sheer insanity. And if we were to fulfil such a demand, others would start making similar demands. In other words, people want God to become a toy for their imagination, and keep changing His attributes like an impersonator (God forbid) so that everyone's fancy should be satisfied.

مَا قَدَرُوا اللَّهَ حَقَّ قَدْرِهِ ¹

The people have not comprehended the attributes of
Allah at all.

Do try to understand that the less subtle a thing, the easier it can
be observed through physical senses, and the more subtle it is, the
harder it is for the physical senses to experience it. It is for this
reason that when we try to learn about subtle things we have to
depend on their properties and their behaviour, rather than on
direct observation. How then is it possible for God—who is not
only Himself the most Subtle Being but is also the Creator of
every subtle thing—to be seen by our physical eyes? The objection of the critics that they will not believe in God until they see
Him with their eyes is, therefore, absurd. It would imply that the
critic either believes God to be a corporeal being, or at least wants
God to assume a corporeal form so that he can be absolutely sure
by seeing Him with his own eyes. But the trouble is that there are
millions of blind people in this world. Would they too not have
the right to demand that God should assume some other material form so that they may taste, smell or feel Him? Does this not
amount to ridiculing God? How shameful for a man who pro-
fesses to have a mind and a heart!

If someone says that he would not believe in God unless he
sees Him with his own eyes, all I should say is that if God could
be seen with one's eyes, He would not be worth believing in at all.
This is because in such a case many of His other attributes would
be falsified. He is Incorporeal, for instance, but in this case He

---

1. *Sūrah al-Ḥajj*, 22:75.

would become corporeal. He is Infinite but would become finite
and so on and so forth. Moreover, if God were to adopt a corporeal and finite form for your sake, what is there to guarantee that
you would not reject Him saying that you do not believe in a corporeal and finite God?

O God, how very Holy, Adorable and Perfect You are! Each
attribute of Yours is guarded by another of Your attributes.
When anyone attacks any one of Your attributes, Your other
attributes—like vigilant and dutiful sentries—put such a person to shame. We have seen how a critic tried to create doubt
concerning God's attribute of being Hidden, but His attributes
of being Incorporeal and Infinite came forward at once and did
away with the objection.

The Beauty of God lies in His being Hidden from our physical
eyes and yet being apparent to us; He is Subtle but remains more
evident and perceptible than material things. Unfortunate indeed
is he who does not comprehend this subtle truth, for he stands on
the brink of disaster.

In summary, the perfection of God Almighty demands that
He be Subtle and Hidden from the physical eyes. This should not
cause any uncertainty about His existence, for there are far more
certain and conclusive ways available to recognise Him.

My dear brothers, pray do not deprive yourself of the precious
bounty of faith on account of such baseless misconceptions. Will
you follow the footsteps of those who believed in the magnetic
and electric forces though they could not see them; and accepted
the sovereignty of space and time and bowed down before lust
and anger; but when it came to offering their Lord and Master the

tribute of their love and servitude, they refused? Surely you will
not do such a thing!!

Why Should We Inquire about God?

Now we come to the proper subject matter. Anyone who does not
believe in God could naturally ask why he should waste time and
energy in finding out whether or not there is a God. Therefore, it
is vital to answer this question at the very outset.

Let us first understand that there are only two ways of finding out if we need to do something or not. First, we see whether
what we need offers us any benefit. If so, we adopt it, otherwise,
we abandon it. Second, we consider whether it is something by
ignoring which we disadvantage ourselves. If so, we take it on,
otherwise we let it go.

Therefore, if it is established that undertaking a task is beneficial for us or that we risk harm in leaving that particular task, then
every wise person will conclude that it is not only appropriate but
essential to undertake that task. Using the same principle, we can
determine the degree of importance of any particular task. That is
to say, if we expect great benefit from undertaking a task or risk a
great loss by leaving it, it becomes increasingly necessary for us to
undertake it.

In view of these two principles, let us answer the question as
to whether we need to inquire into the existence of God. If it is
proven that God does exist, then: 1) Is there any benefit for us to
believe in Him? 2) Do we disadvantage ourselves in any way by
denying Him? Now, the answer to these questions would depend

on how the question is put before us. If it is presented to us in such a way that it makes little difference to us whether we believe in God or not, then it would merely be a hypothetical question, and everyone, with the exception of those who are interested in such hypothesis would be justified in refusing to go into this research. People would of course want to concentrate upon matters which directly benefit or harm them. For example, if someone were to claim that he had discovered a new star billions of light years from the earth and which did not have the slightest effect on our solar system or on our planet—we would expect none but astronomers to be interested in it. But if someone were to claim that he has discovered a new drug which could rejuvenate the human body, remarkably prolong life to an average of 150-200 years, and delay the effects of old age, and if the man who makes such a claim is no charlatan, then the whole world would be captivated by the idea. Were such a claim to be true it could affect every man's life significantly.

When we return to the question of God, we find that there are three sources which put the question before us: 1) Human Nature, 2) Reason, 3) Religion.

I shall first of all take up human nature. Everyone who has a mind prone to analysis and whose true nature is not covered by veils of darkness and ignorance, does occasionally feel in his heart of hearts that there is likely to be a God who has created him and who governs this universe. Likewise, if we did not come into this universe by ourselves and if there is someone who has created us, then would there not be a purpose in the mind of the Creator? Though I do not imply that human nature also provides answers to these questions, what is certain is that it does bring them up in our minds and in such a way that we cannot dismiss them as irrelevant. One has the right to investigate and come to the conclusion that there is no God and that this world and all that exists has really come into existence from nothing and is running on its own, but after all these questions no one can deny the right to research this matter.

The same is true of human reason, which, even though it might eventually come to the conclusion that there is no God, poses these questions to us very forcefully. In fact, it presents these questions much more clearly and elaborately than human nature does. It warns us to reflect and consider lest there be a God who has sent us to this world for a particular purpose and lest we should die without knowing Him and being unaware of the purpose of our creation. We must therefore wake up and try to find Him! We have not come to this world merely to eat and drink and fulfil our sensual desires, and to leave behind a progeny that plays the same role in the world as we have done! Let us open our eyes and reflect whether we have come into existence out of nothingness. Is the complex and comprehensive system of your body its own creator? Is the cosmos, with its intelligently organised and balanced system operating throughout its length and breadth, merely a result of chance? If this is not the case, and this system is in fact the manifestation of the great power of a Supreme Being, then is it possible that He has produced this vast universe merely as a toy to please His eyes so that when He has had enough of it, He should destroy it with one stroke of His mighty hand and set about creating a new one?

Is it not likely that there is a purpose for man's life? Is it not likely that he shall be answerable for his deeds? These are the questions, which arise in every man's mind. Now, ask yourself honestly, are these questions so irrelevant and meaningless that we should not even bother to think about them? I do not ask you to answer these questions, as their answers can vary according to the investigative prowess of every individual, and no honest researcher can tell beforehand what the outcome of his investigation will be. But one thing I can say for certain: The manner in which these questions come up in our minds demands that we should not waste any time before trying to find out their answers. We should not rest for a moment until our independent and honest investigation has led us to a final conclusion.

In summary, human nature and intellect both present this issue—the existence of God—in such a manner that provokes us undeniably to seek the truth about the existence of God. Is it really irrelevant for us to seek an answer to the question of whether or not we have a Creator? And is it so irrelevant to ask, 'If someone has created us, who and where is He, and what are His attributes?' Does it not matter that we learn—if we have a Creator—what is the purpose of our creation and how can we attain it? If these questions are relevant, and certainly they are, then no wise person can refuse to seek their answers.

Last, but not least, this question is also raised by religion. All religions in the world invariably raise the question of God Almighty before us. God and His attributes form the very core of the teachings of every religion and billions of their followers believe their religions to have originated from God and to be based upon the Divine Word which has been revealed throughout the ages and has kept the world illuminated. Though some teachings of these religions have been interpolated and corrupted,

they were originally based on Divine Revelation. Hence, religions
provide much more detailed, clear, and definite descriptions of
the Being of God, than human nature or human reason. In other
words, the brief message contained in human nature and reason
has been elaborated by revelation. Human nature and reason only
hint at the possibility of the existence of God, but religion tells us
as a matter of absolute certainty that we do have a God, who is our
Creator and Master and who has sent us to this world for a special purpose. The different religions may differ on many of their
teachings, but they are in total agreement on the basic points. For
example, they agree that the universe has a Creator and Master
with complete control over our lives and that He has ordained
some purpose for our lives and also taught us the ways and means
to achieve it. Religions teach that death is not the end of man's
life, rather there is another life after death in which we shall get
a reward for the deeds of our present existence. This unanimous
testimony of all religions brings forth the question of Almighty
God in such a way that we are compelled to investigate and find
answers. If all the above claims made by different religions are
true, then being unaware of God is the greatest loss we can possibly suffer in this world, for such ignorance would mean that we
have lived our lives in vain. On the other hand, all religions claim
that recognition of God and a strong relationship with Him is
greater than all the gains which we can possibly acquire in this
world. Establishing this relationship means that we have achieved
the goal for which we were created, and that we have fulfilled the
purpose of our lives. Hence we conclude that the search for God
is so important that no sensible person can afford to ignore it for
an instant.

After discussing the unanimous testimony of religions, I would like to say something in particular about the teachings of Islam. Islam tells us that we have One God, who is our Creator and Master, and that He has brought us into existence from nothingness and it is He who controls our lives. He wants us to achieve a higher status. He has made all kinds of provisions for our welfare. Islam says that we have One God who is Gracious—i.e. He takes care of all our needs and He provides us with our requirements without our asking or striving for them. Islam says that we have One God who is Merciful—i.e. He produces the best reward for our efforts and does not let them go in vain. Islam says that we have One God who is the 'Lord of the Day of Judgment'—i.e. He pronounces reward or punishment for our deeds. He warns us of the consequences of following the wrong path, so that we do not become heedless and forget the goal of our life that He has ordained for us. One day we will be held answerable before Him. Islam says that we have One God who is Most Forgiving—when we strive in His path, He forgives our mistakes and shortcomings and protects us from their ill consequences. Islam says that we have One God who is the Acceptor of repentance—i.e. when we feel true remorse for our sins and turn towards the right path with true sincerity and wholeheartedly pledge to get rid of consequences of sins and to do good deeds, God too comes to our help, accepts our repentance and covers our sins with His mercy. Islam says that we have One God who is All-Powerful—i.e. nothing is beyond His power, no matter how difficult or impossible it may seem to us. Islam says that we have One God who is All-Hearing—i.e. He hears the call of everyone and there is no voice that does not reach Him. Islam says that we have a God who is All-Knowing—i.e. no

deed or thought, whether overt or covert, is beyond the sphere
of His knowledge. Islam says that we have One God who is the
Helper—i.e. at times of crisis and difficulty, He comes to our aid,
provided we have a true relationship with Him. Islam says that we
have One God who is Eternal—i.e. He has always been and shall
always be; time does not have any effect on Him. Islam says that
we have One God who is the Most Majestic—i.e. He is the perfect blend of all that is perfect and all that is good, and He alone
is worthy of our adoration. Islam says that we have One God who
is very Loving—i.e. He loves those who establish personal communion with Him, and He shows more love and loyalty towards
them than any other lover. Islam says that we have One God who
Speaks—i.e. He bestows His speech upon those who have established communion with Him. Though He is invisible to our eyes
by virtue of being the Most Subtle, He sprinkles the pure water of
his loving speech upon those whose hearts are ablaze with the fire
of His love, lest it should burn them to ashes. How beautifully the
Promised Messiah[as], the Founder of the Ahmadiyya Movement,
has expressed:

میں تو مر کر خاک ہوتا گر نہ ہوتا تیرا لطف   پھر خدا جانے کہاں یہ پھینک دی جاتی غبار

But for Your Grace, I would have perished and turned to dust;
God only knows where this dust might then have been discarded.

Dear ones! This is the God presented by Islam. I do not ask you to
believe in Him. All I say is that these are the attributes of our God
as proclaimed by Islam. Islam goes further and proclaims that we
can find this God if we seek and strive for Him. Do you now consider this search and investigation to be useless and irrelevant? If

you have a mind that ponders and a sensitive heart, you will never consider this quest futile.

Awake my friends, and strive to find your God! Rush towards the fountain of life. Hasten towards that treasure which will set you free from the shackles of the world. I cannot describe in words what you will attain were you to find Him. Listen to these holy verses of the Promised Messiah[as]:

تُجھے سب زور و قدرت ہے خدایا تُجھے پایا ہر اِک مقصد کو پایا

Lord! All might and power belongs to You;
By finding You, we attained fulfilment of all our desires.

ہر اک عاشق نے ہے اک بت بنایا ہمارے دل میں ہے دلبر سمایا

Every lover has carved for himself an idol;
But our Beloved alone has captivated our hearts.

وہی آرام جاں اور دل کو بھایا وہی جس کو کہیں رب البرایا

He alone is the Comfort of our soul and the Darling of our heart;
He is the One whom we call the Lord of Creation.

ہوا ظاہر وہ مجھ پر بالایادی فسبحان الذی اخزی الاعادی

He has dawned upon me through His blessings;
Holy is He who has humbled my opponents.

مجھے اُس یار سے پیوندِ جاں ہے وہی جنّت وہی دارالاماں ہے

I am bound to that Friend with my very life;
He alone is Paradise and the Ultimate Refuge.

بیاں اس کا کروں طاقت کہاں ہے   محبت کا تو اک دریا رواں ہے

To glorify Him, wherefrom can I seek the power?
A sea of love flows in my heart.

یہ کیا احساں ترے ہیں میرے ہادی   فسبحان الذی اخزی الاعادی

How great is Your Benevolence, O my Guide;
Holy is He who has humbled my opponents.

تری رحمت کی کچھ قلت نہیں ہے   تھی اس سے کوئی ساعت نہیں ہے

There is no limit to Your Mercy;
Not a moment is devoid of Your Grace.

شمارِ فضل اور رحمت نہیں ہے   مجھے اب شکر کی طاقت نہیں ہے

There is no counting Your Blessings and Your Mercy;
I no longer have the strength to thank You enough.

یہ کیا احساں ہیں تیرے میرے ہادی   فسبحان الذی اخزی الاعادی

How great is Your Beneficence, O my Guide;
Holy is He who has humbled my opponents.

If you try to find your Lord and fail, then your failure itself proves that your life has no purpose because something that has come into existence by accident can have no real purpose. If such were the case, then your existence has been pointless. Would this defeat not be better than all the successes you achieve in your aimless life? But, let me assure you, you will never fail in this search. Set off in this quest, therefore, with sincerity, love and true zeal, and

you will soon find the pleasant winds of success welcoming you.
Have you not heard these verses of the Promised Messiah[as]?

تجھے دنیا میں ہے کس نے پکارا   کہ پھر خالی گیا قسمت کا مارا

Who in the world ever besought You,
  And returned empty handed, the unfortunate one!

تو پھر ہے کس قدر اس کو سہارا   کہ جس کا تو ہی ہے سب سے پیارا

How assured must then he be,
  Whose greatest love is You alone.

Methods of Inquiry into God's Existence

Now, I will describe briefly what methods to use in our investigation concerning [the existence of] God; for, unless we know
the proper way to look for a particular thing, we are unlikely to
succeed in finding it. We may waste all our efforts by adopting the
wrong method. A person cannot successfully dig a water well until
he selects a particular plot of land and digs perpendicularly in a
specific manner. If one tries digging horizontally along the earth,
for even two hundred miles, they will be unsuccessful as this
method is incorrect! Therefore, it would be absurd to complain
that all this hard work and labour resulted in nothing; this will be
unacceptable for any sensible person. Thus, mere hard work and
effort do not matter much, unless appropriately channelled. You
see, to achieve anything in this world, we need to follow a proper
method in accordance with the laws of nature. Without adhering
to the correct process, a particular task cannot be accomplished.

Likewise, in religious matters, there is a way and a method specified for every purpose and one cannot achieve that purpose without adopting the right method—no matter how hard one may toil
or deliberate. This set of laws is absolutely to our advantage, as
without them it will be impossible for man to progress intellec-
tually and practically. Suppose there were no laws in this world
and man were to achieve anything merely by wishing it: What
then would happen to this world? Would ignorance, slothfulness,
indolence, and inexperience not prevail instead of knowledge, dil-
igence, effort, and experience? Would there remain any distinction and difference between the scholarly and the ignorant, the
industrious and the indolent, the hard-working and the slothful,
the experienced and the novice? Would this not block the intellectual progress of man? Would it not cause irreparable damage
to man's elevated moral status? Think hard and realize that all the
physical, material, academic, practical, moral, and spiritual progress that you see around you is due only to the fact that the universe is operating in accordance with a set of laws. For every purpose there is a specified way, without which it cannot be achieved.
If you ignore the laws of nature, this will detriment your progress
and block the progress of human intellect. Human beings, who
have been called the most eminent of all created things, would
fall lower than the most despised of all creation. Therefore, do not
regard the law of nature as an obstacle in your way, for these are the
devices granted by the Creator of the universe for you to utilise in
order to reach the pinnacles of knowledge and accomplishment.
Consider them the sun of guidance, ordained by your Gracious
Master to illumine for you the avenues of future progress. This is
a test designed to distinguish the scholarly from the ignorant, the

active from the inactive, the experienced from the novice, and the industrious from the slothful.

The Role of Intention in the Field of Research

First of all, it should be realised that intention has a great role to play in how one proceeds with their chosen task. The same task undertaken with different intentions leads to different outcomes and effects. In short, intention plays a big role in every task one undertakes and the reality of intention inevitably impacts the outcome. This effect is not hypothetical and imaginary but definite and real. For instance, take the case of one who is employed to work under an officer. He obeys him only because he is his superior, but has no personal interest in carrying out his orders and has no personal relationship of love with him, nor is he impressed by his competence and capability. In such a case, he would obey merely because he is legally bound to do so and he would comply with his orders to fulfil his contractual obligations. One will not see any zeal, fervour, or interest in his performance. However, if the same person had a personal bond of loyalty with the officer, admiration for his competence and capability, and interest in his orders, then his obedience would acquire a totally different character, and his approach to the job would be absolutely exceptional. All his actions would show zeal, fervour, and personal interest. This difference is because of different intentions; though obedience is carried out under both circumstances, the difference in intentions has made a world of difference in the approach to work.

The same applies to inquiring about God. A philosopher researches, and so does the seeker, with the same objective—i.e. to find God—but with completely different intentions. The philosopher carries out his research with the intention of finding out whether or not there is a Creator of this universe by studying the universe; his intention is solely to gain intellectual capital. Beyond His existence, he is not interested in learning about His attributes, His relationship with His servants, the relationship His servants should have with Him, or the means to reach Him. He does not desire a relationship with Him, nor does he long for His nearness, nor seek His friendship, nor is he anxious to reach Him or to learn and comply with His will. He wants only to fulfil his academic research. On the other hand, the one who seeks God with true zeal desires to have a true bond with God, wishes to attain His friendship and love, yearns to find Him, and aspires to attain ways that will earn God's pleasure. Can the search of the two be alike? No, never. So, first of all, one must purify their intention and search as a seeker and not as a philosopher, and cultivate the eagerness and passion required for the search of truth. Milk would not begin to flow from the breasts of a mother for her infant were the infant to present a serious and appropriate face to the mother and ask the mother to show him whether or not milk is present for his sustenance; rather, milk flows readily and freely for a baby who seeks it with the agony of hunger and cries for it. At such a time, even if the mother should wish, she cannot stop the milk from flowing, and this milk becomes a source of nourishment for the baby and saves him from dying. Similarly, God does not manifest Himself to a philosopher; rather, He keeps away from him because He does not want to become a plaything, to be toyed with by the imaginations of the philosophers. In contrast, God Himself comes to the seeker; God is more loving and faithful than a mother and does not wish His true seeker to perish in the darkness [of ignorance]. It is amazing that both seeker and philosopher seek God but He turns away from the philosopher and hurries towards the seeker!

So, O my dear ones! In your search for God, never tread the path of philosophers, for you will never find God that way. The search for Him in this way is fruitless anyway because if, after finding God, we do nothing about it, then what is the point of seeking Him? Why should we spend our time, attention, and energy just to confirm whether or not God exists? This will not help us at all; rather, it will be damaging, as remaining unmindful after finding Him will make us guilty of two crimes. God will never reveal His Countenance to us as a result of this type of effort. He will only manifest Himself to us when He sees that we want to reach Him with genuine eagerness, our objective is to benefit from the blessings of His nearness, and we wish to establish a personal relationship with Him in order to attain the heights of progress—which is, after all, the purpose of human life. Therefore, develop true eagerness and passion, so that your efforts may be fruitful and your labour may achieve the purpose. The Promised Messiah[as] says:

کوئی راہ نزدیک تر راہِ محبت سے نہیں   طے کریں اس راہ سے سالک ہزاروں دشتِ خار

There is no path nearer than the path of love,
  Following which the seekers cross countless thorny deserts.

اس کے پانے کا یہی اے دوستو اک راز ہے   کیمیا ہے جس سے ہاتھ آجائے گا زر بے شمار

Love is the secret to reach Him, O friends;

    It is the alchemy that will make you wealthy beyond imagination.

تیر تاثیرِ محبت کا خطا جاتا نہیں   تیر اندازو نہ ہونا سُت اس میں زینہار

The arrow of love's effect never misses its target;

    O my archers, slacken not for a moment.

ہے یہی اک آگ تا تم کو بچائے آگ سے   ہے یہی پانی کہ نکلیں جس سے صدہا آبشار

This is the fire that shall protect you from all fire;

    This is the water from which flow countless springs.

اس سے خود آکر ملے گا تم سے وہ یارِ ازل   اس سے تم عرفانِ حق سے پہنو گے پھولوں کے ہار

It is love that will make that Eternal Friend come to you by Himself;

    It is this that shall adorn you with garlands of true knowledge.

And he says:

فلسفی کز عقل می جوید ترا دیوانہ ہست   دور تر ہست از خردہا آں راہِ پنہانِ تو

Whoever wants to find God through mere intellect is certainly mad,

    Because the hidden ways of His access are beyond the reach of mere intellect.

Two Levels of Belief in God

The next point I wish to make is that, on the one hand, the Being of God is sublime, and cannot be seen by man's physical eyes due to His being infinite and extremely subtle; on the other, our faith cannot be perfected or cannot be of any use unless we attain belief in God—at least as much as the faith we have in the material things of this world. Therefore, God has decreed in His wisdom that man should make progress towards Him to a certain level and then God will Himself descend towards man and raise man towards Himself. In other words, God has divided belief in two parts: one which man can achieve with the help of his own intellect, and one which is beyond the reach of reason alone, and attaining this part of faith requires Heavenly support to assist dry logic. God states in the Holy Quran:

$$\text{لَا تُدْرِكُهُ الْأَبْصَارُ ۖ وَهُوَ يُدْرِكُ الْأَبْصَارَ ۖ وَهُوَ اللَّطِيفُ الْخَبِيرُ}^{1}$$

This means that human eyes are unable to see God or perceive His true Being. Therefore, God has made this arrangement, whereby He Himself reaches out to man; that is to say, He has Himself put in place a system that helps man appreciate and comprehend the knowledge of His existence. For, God is beyond the reach of man's physical eyes yet He is *Khabīr* [All-Aware] and knows that it is not possible for man to have a spiritual life without recognising Him. Therefore, God provides means from Himself that enable man to recognise Him, despite God being *Laṭīf* [Subtle] and Unseen.

---

1. *Sūrah al-Anʿām*, 6:104.

So لَا تُدْرِكُهُ الْأَبْصَارُ [Eyes cannot reach Him] has been paired with
the Divine attribute of *Laṭīf* [Subtle, Incomprehensible] to show
that logic alone cannot take one to God, as He is *Laṭīf;* while وَهُوَ
يُدْرِكُ الْأَبْصَارَ [He reaches the eyes] has been paired with His attribute
of *Khabīr* [All-Aware]; i.e. He makes it possible for Himself to
be recognised because He is *Khabīr.* The two former attributes,
لَا تُدْرِكُهُ الْأَبْصَارُ وَهُوَ يُدْرِكُ الْأَبْصَارَ [Eyes cannot reach Him, but He reaches
the eyes], are logical outcomes of His latter two attributes *al-Laṭīf*
[the Subtle, Incomprehensible] and *al-Khabīr* [the All-Aware].

Now, on the one hand we have in the Holy Quran the teaching stated above; and on the other, we see the Holy Quran directs
people, time and again, to reflect upon this universe, the heavens,
the earth, and other creation, and ponder whether this entire universe with its amazingly wise system could come into existence by
mere chance. Certainly not! Rather all of this organisation cries
out that there ought certainly to be someone who brought this
entire system into being. Thus the Holy Quran repeatedly draws
the attention of man to contemplate the issue of God's existence
and to discover the Creator through the study of His creation.
This line of argument suggests that reason is enough and needs no
heavenly assistance, whereas the verse referred to above tells us that
the perception of God is beyond human capacity and, therefore,
God Himself makes such arrangements, with the help of which
man can acquire knowledge and understanding of God. The two
statements seem to contradict each other, but on reflection there
is no contradiction and both statements are correct in their own
right. It is true that man can find his way to God with the help of
reason, and it is also true that reason alone cannot grant knowledge and cognizance of God, but requires heavenly signs and

corroboratory evidence in order to achieve these. The solution to
this enigma is as follows: As stated above, belief in God is divided
into two levels. The elementary level is one that is attainable with
logic only. The second level (and that in fact is the stage called
īmān billāh [belief in God] in religious terminology) is one that
is unattainable with reason alone and God Himself grants special
Divine help to reach it. The first degree of belief, which is attainable by logic and reasoning, can lead us only to the conclusion
that there *ought to be* a Creator and Master of this universe, as
this earth and the heavens could not have come into existence by
mere chance, and so on. The second degree of belief leads one to
the conclusion that there indeed *is* a Creator and Master of this
universe, with multiple attributes, who can be found by adopting
certain means. That is to say, the first stage is that of 'ought to be'
and second that of 'is'.

Now think hard, mere reason and logic can never lead us to
the stage of 'is'; reason and logic can only instil an understanding
within ourselves that there ought to be a God. That is to say, logic
on its own cannot grant us faith in God, but indeed logic can prepare us to accept faith; logic, as it stands, cannot show us God but
can point us from afar in His direction; it cannot unite us with
our God but can open the door for such a meeting; logic on its
own cannot grant us the satisfaction concerning the existence of
God, but can grant us the eagerness that is required to attain this
satisfaction. Thus, logic and reasoning can grant us certainty that
there *should be* a God, but cannot create certainty in our hearts
concerning God. This is beyond the capacity of logic and reason-
ing. This is explained in the Divine philosophy of لَا تُدْرِكُهُ الْأَبْصَارُ [the
eyes cannot reach Him]. Therefore, logic and reasoning require

special Divine support in order to progress from 'should be' to 'is'. In other words, the limited vision of reason stops at the 'ought to be' stage and cannot proceed further until granted special insight by God. When such insight is granted, this unveils the reality about the existence of God. Those who were unable to recognise God before are enabled to behold the brilliant countenance of the Creator. As man attains greater and greater nearness to God, his comprehension of God becomes sharper and this knowledge and cognizance go on improving. There is no limit to this nearness or end to this knowledge and cognizance, for God is an Infinite Being and the cognizance of an Infinite Being cannot be finite or limited. That is why—along with every common man—*Ḥaḍrat Khātamur-Rusul* [the Seal of the Messengers], peace and blessings of Allah be on him, who was *Sarwar-e-Kā'ināt* [the Leader of Mankind], offered the prayer:

$$رَبِّ زِدْنِیْ عِلْمًا ¹$$

Meaning that, 'O my Lord, increase me in knowledge'. And yet he is the one whom God directed to say:

$$اَنَا سَیِّدُ وَلَدِ اٰدَمَ وَ لَا فَخْرَ$$

Meaning that, I am the chief of all men but I take no pride in it. And about whom God said the following:

---

1. *Sūrah Ṭā Hā*, 20:115.

دَنَا فَتَدَلّٰى فَكَانَ قَابَ قَوْسَيْنِ اَوۡ اَدۡنٰى [1]

Meaning that, this servant of Ours came close to Us, and became so near that he lost himself in Us. اللّٰهم صلّ على محمّدٍ وبارك وسلّم [O Allah, bless and prosper and shower Thy peace on Muhammad].

It is sad that most people believe that they have achieved all that there is to be achieved by attaining the elementary stage of belief. Even sadder is the fact that most people think that they have found God if their search for God leads them only to the stage of 'ought to be'. There is no doubt that 'ought to be' is a stepping stone towards the stage of 'is' and, in the spiritual world, the preliminary awareness of God begins at this point. But if man stops at this stage, believing it to be the end-all and the purpose, this can prove to be extremely dangerous and disastrous for him. Many a time, stopping the search for God at this point can push a man forever into the darkness of atheism, and he dies in this state of ignorance. Because when he sees that despite all his efforts he failed to find God, and at most reached the notion that there 'ought to be' a God, dismayed, he considers his reason's counsel as a deception, and ends up denying the existence of God. His condition is similar to that of a man who finds the door to a room bolted from the inside and waits outside, believing that there ought to be someone inside the room since the door can be bolted only from the inside. If such a person receives no response to his knocking, calling, and shouting for a long time, this will create doubts and suspicions in his heart—perhaps the door became locked due to some unknown cause, or maybe the one who bolted

---

1. *Sūrah an-Najm*, 53:9–10.

it died inside, and so on—ultimately, he would totally despair, and return believing that no one was inside.

So, concerning God, if the 'ought to be' stage of belief does not lead to the 'is' stage of belief, then the end result is nothing but despair and atheism; for, those granted with the ability to ponder will find it impossible to stop at that stage—they will either proceed further or after a while turn back in despair. However, it is a pity that there are many people in the world (nay, they are in the majority) whose eyes are covered with such veils of heedlessness that upon reaching the 'ought to be' stage they become content and believe they have recognised God and have achieved what they had set out to achieve. That is to say, out of their naivety, lack of awareness, and ignorance, they think it suffices to know that their ought to be a Creator of this universe; they do not determinedly explore that if there ought to be a Creator, then does He really exist or not, and if there is one, who is He, where is He, what are His attributes, how can we establish a bond with Him, and how can we know if He has any connection with us? Such people neither worry about making progress in their knowledge of God, nor turn back because of their false sense of security, till death overtakes them. They die in a state believing that they have reached their destination whereas they are still treading the path to God. Most of the people who claim to believe in God these days fall in this category. Alas! Unfortunate man! You traversed some distance in the weak and dim light of reason; but when the time came for you to bask in the rays of the Divine spiritual sun and—having initially recognised your Lord and Master from afar—to then (rather than stumbling) run towards Him eagerly till you become so near Him that His Holy attributes, like a mother's lap, envelop you, you stepped aside and sat along the track in the dim light of reason, and spent your life there, thinking that you have found God. I cannot understand how your heart—endowed with such thirst for certainty by the Creator of nature, which cannot be satiated without true conviction, and wherein a fire of love and affection has been kindled that cannot be extinguished without the water of Divine love—find satisfaction without achieving its purpose? If you are not deceiving others, you are certainly deceived yourself. Remember that in some cases being deceived can bring you into the fold of criminals. Therefore, fear God and do not become the cause of your own destruction and the misguidance of others by sitting on the wayside.

LOGICAL ARGUMENTS FOR THE EXISTENCE OF GOD

Cautious Approach

Now I will put forward some logical arguments for the existence of God. As stated above, these arguments take us only to the 'ought to be' stage. To proceed any further we will need a different kind of evidence, which, God willing, will be discussed later. Before these logical arguments, I would like to present one point as a precaution. It is no secret that many times we take measures which are precautionary and not essential. For instance, when camping in a jungle at night, we arrange for a night watchman for our protection, even if the dangers of wild beasts and thieves are not immediately imminent. This is because logic dictates that arranging for a guard will not harm us, and if there is an unexpected danger then security at night will undoubtedly be most helpful to us. In short, it is normal for us to undertake precautionary measures and everyone agrees that such precautionary measures are necessary and beneficial.

Thus, when we ponder the existence of God based on this principle, our reason concludes that it is certainly safer and more prudent to believe in God than to deny Him. If there is no God and this universe came into existence by chance, obviously our belief in God can do us no harm. However, if there is indeed a God, our belief will certainly be useful and beneficial. There can only be two logical answers to this question: either this universe came into existence all by itself and is self-propelled and God is a false notion (God forbid), or the universe has a Creator and Master who has created it and is managing it. Our reason does not suggest any third possibility. Now, if we deny the existence of God, the possibility that He might exist potentially poses serious problems for us; whereas if we believe in a God that does not actually exist, this has no dangerous implications whatsoever for us.

$$\text{فَاَىُّ الْفَرِيقَيْنِ اَحَقُّ بِالْاَمْنِ ۚ اِنْ كُنْتُمْ تَعْلَمُوْنَ}^{1}$$

Meaning that, which of the two parties then has greater right to security, if indeed you know—the one that denies or the one that believes? Thus, it is established that belief in God is prudent because there is no harm in it, whereas denying the existence of God can potentially be harmful.

It is narrated that someone asked Ḥaḍrat Ali[ra] for proof God's existence. Seeing that the man was a simple man, he replied: It is enough for you to realise that if there is no God, the believers and

---

1. *Sūrah al-Anʿām*, 6:82.

non-believers are all the same and no one has anything to lose. However, if there is indeed a God, then the deniers would be in grave trouble. This rationale satisfied the man and he asked no further question.

What is the harm in believing in God even if He does not exist? What must we give up if we believe in God? Belief in God requires you to refrain from adultery, murder, theft, robbery, falsehood, deceit, fraud, etc.—the actions that nature, logic, and the law of the land want you to give up anyway! So, what can you possibly lose by believing in God? This belief does not at all bar you from fulfilling any of your just desires in a fair manner. You are free to eat and drink, sleep and wake, sit and stand, play and relax, read and write, do worldly jobs, earn money, establish friendships, make homes, get married, and have children—belief in God does not stop you from any of these. Belief in God stops you only from acts that are harmful and detrimental to yourselves or others. Refraining from such acts is supported by your own nature, reason, and societal and governmental laws. So, what do you have to lose by believing in God? You may ask why you should believe in God without evidence. My answer is that you should adopt this as one more of the numerous precautionary measures you take in this world. In any case, when there is a possibility of gain and no risk of loss in believing, but there is no possibility of benefit and a risk of harm in denial, then think: which option is nearer to peace and prudence? Obviously, those who deny God only do so because according to them there is no evidence of God's existence, not because they have evidence that God does not exist. In such a case then, every sensible person, being circumspect, would decide that it is safer to believe in God. To summarise, if there is no God, then all are equal and belief in God is unlikely to cause any harm. However, if there is indeed a God, then the believers will be at an advantage and disbelievers will have to think for themselves about their fate!

One may question the benefit of faith that is based on precaution rather than faith based upon earnestness. Indeed this is not true faith, but it is better than having no faith. Someone with such faith will maintain at least some bond with God, which in due course may serve as a stepping stone to true faith. Moreover, such belief can at times motivate one to do good deeds. In any case, however defective such belief may be, it is certainly better than no belief. There is no reason to deprive oneself of the faith that is based on precaution, as explained above.

Argument Based on Fitrah, i.e. Human Nature

Now I come to the main arguments proving the existence of God. The first argument that I want to present is based on human nature. While discussing the need to investigate God's existence I had mentioned that our nature raises this question from within us: Is there a Creator and Master of the universe or not? Therefore, we cannot ignore this question. Human nature not only raises this question but also answers it. Those who are accustomed to listening to their nature do hear it.

What is meant by *fitrah*? One must understand this clearly, otherwise it will be difficult to understand what the voice of *fitrah* truly means. *Fitrah* is an Arabic word derived from *fitar*. Thus it is said:

فُلَانٌ فَطَرَ الْأَمْرَ اَیْ اِخْتَرَعَه، وَابْتَدَءَه، وَاَنْشَاءَه

Thus, *faṭara* means to make something that did not exist before; he originated it and—having brought it into existence from nothing—enabled it to progress further in life. On this basis the lexicologists have translated *fiṭrah* as:

الصفة التى یتصف بها كلّ مولود فى اوّل زمان خلقته۔

That is, *fiṭrah* is the name given to those qualities invested in every child from the moment of its creation. According to this definition, human *fiṭrah* [nature] means the features and characteristics which are not developed under the influence of environmental factors, but are endowed in man, through the process of creation and in his nature, in order to enable him to explore the avenues of progress. Everything has certain characteristics known as its natural traits. The sum total of such characteristics is *fiṭrah*. These characteristics and attributes are either suppressed or augmented under the influence of environmental factors and on that depends the progress or decline of the person. Everyone can analyse themselves and find out which way their inborn qualities are heading. For instance, truthfulness is an innate quality; i.e. it is an innate feature of man to utter only that which is in accordance with the facts. Therefore, every child initially conforms to this innate quality. However, when he sees that his parents sometimes become upset when they see him doing a particular thing which he very much likes to do, the desire to do that act grows in him, but fearing their displeasure he tries to hide it from them. That is the first veil that befalls his *fiṭrah*. Gradually he is prepared to carry on with his desired act and not only hides it from his parents but on their questioning tells a lie and denies the act. Thus the innate quality—to tell the truth in all cases—continues to be suppressed under the veils of darkness till, as it were, he totally forgets his *fiṭrah*. At this stage, it is said that his *fiṭrah* has died. Though, in fact, *fiṭrah* never dies; it only becomes obscured and veiled under external influences. The same applies to other innate emotions. For instance, love, hate, clemency, wrath, forgiveness, revenge, bravery, fear, chastity, lust, desire for progress and hatred for decline, and other similar emotions are naturally ingrained in human *fiṭrah,* but external influences suppress or augment them. That is to say, these emotions can be taken to the highest or lowest extremes, and at times practiced in moderation.

Given these circumstances, therefore, the voice of *fiṭrah* represents a very delicate and difficult issue. Apart from those whose emotions are in a state of moderation, people are generally deceived about their own *fiṭrah*. In spite of all that, undoubtedly, *fiṭrah* is an undeniable reality. Each innate quality makes a demand that is called its voice. For instance, truthfulness is an innate quality and it demands that one should describe an event exactly as it happened, neither contrary to it nor anything additional. This demand is called the voice of *fiṭrah*. To keep this innate voice alive, Allah the Exalted says in the Holy Quran:

فَاَقِمْ وَجْهَكَ لِلدِّيْنِ حَنِيْفًا ۚ فِطْرَتَ اللّٰهِ الَّتِیْ فَطَرَ النَّاسَ عَلَیْهَا ۚ [1]

---

1. *Sūrah ar-Rūm,* 30:31.

That is, O man! Stay focused on moderation so as to maintain the nature according to which Allah has fashioned mankind.

Now, everyone should look into his inner self to discover whether or not his *fiṭrah* tells him anything about the existence of God. In solitude, let him ask himself: Do I owe my existence to mere chance or to creation by a Higher Being? In response, in the absence of any preconceived notion based on logic, does he hear the voice of *fiṭrah* or not? The Holy Quran says:

وَ اِذْ اَخَذَ رَبُّكَ مِنْ بَنِیْۤ اٰدَمَ مِنْ ظُهُوْرِهِمْ ذُرِّیَّتَهُمْ وَ اَشْهَدَهُمْ عَلٰۤی اَنْفُسِهِمْ اَلَسْتُ بِرَبِّكُمْ ؕ قَالُوْا بَلٰی ۛۚ شَهِدْنَا ۛۚ اَنْ تَقُوْلُوْا یَوْمَ الْقِیٰمَةِ اِنَّا كُنَّا عَنْ هٰذَا غٰفِلِیْنَ[1]

That is to say, when God started the human race, He made them witnesses against their own selves by asking them: Am I not your Lord? And they said: Indeed, You are our Lord. This He did lest they should say on the Day of Judgement: We never knew anything about God.

This verse means that, when God created man, just as He inscribed in man other qualities and attributes, similarly He inscribed in man's *fiṭrah* that he has a Creator and a Master, of whom he should not remain oblivious. God did this so that no one could present an excuse on the Day of Judgement that they were unaware; otherwise, they would have certainly paid attention to God. In short, like other natural qualities, this special natural quality has also been endowed in us, to realize that we did not come into existence by ourselves and it is the creative power of a Higher Being that has brought us into being. Everyone whose

---

1. *Sūrah al-Aʿrāf,* 7:173.

fiṭrah is not obscured or veiled by external influences will from time to time hear this voice rising from within, that he has a Creator. Even the *fiṭrah* of those who have buried it under the veils of darkness and oblivion, under certain circumstances, suddenly comes alive, and whispers this message into their ears. It has been observed many a time that even an atheist during periods of severe and sudden calamity starts calling out, O Allah or O Rām! One may say that it is because of habit; however, habits develop under the effect of circumstances. But it cannot be said that one who denies God and has insisted on denial for years and who regularly spits venom on believers in his utterances and writings might call on God out of habit. His habit is to revile God and abuse Him—not to call on His help. Thus, the words 'O Allah' or 'O Rām' suddenly coming out of the mouth of a confirmed atheist during a calamity cannot be anything but the voice of *fiṭrah*. In fact, a calamity has the likeness of an earthquake: just as the latter sometimes unearths buried things, a sudden earthquake of calamities sometimes brings out the buried *fiṭrah* of a man and exposes it. The same voice of *fiṭrah*, which could not be heard earlier due to it being buried under thousands of veils, comes to light.

Similarly, we see that when a person becomes older, his ears begin to hear the voices of his *fiṭrah* more clearly. This happens for the same reason that during youth, man is beset by a multitude of diverse neglects and there is an abundance of worldly occupation, and the passions, being astir, usually exceed the bounds of moderation. As one matures, however, passions wane, negligence evaporates, and one has more time at his disposal as worldly commitments decrease. At such a time, one's *fiṭrah* once again makes itself heard. You may go and observe that among the atheists the majority will be youth; however, with the advancement of age, their views begin to change. It has been observed that during old age, many atheists start believing in God, because, with maturity, the voice of their *fiṭrah* compels them to desist from denying the existence of God. Of course, there are always exceptions to this rule, and some people are unable to appreciate the call of their *fiṭrah* even in old age. If under various pressures one keeps suppressing his *fiṭrah* during the mature years, one would succumb to atheism. But, by and large, it is the period of youth when one faces distracting influences and is therefore more likely to succumb to atheism.

It could be argued that this change is due not to the voice of *fiṭrah* but to a fear of death. That is to say, when an old man realises that his death is nigh, he naturally starts fearing and it is this fear that makes him inclined towards God. I say that this point also supports the philosophy of *fiṭrah*. The fear of death is indeed a voice of *fiṭrah;* otherwise, why would the fear of death influence one's atheistic beliefs! A person who regards life as the result of mere chance also considers death in the same way: the end of that life, which had come into being by mere chance, occurs also by chance or for some other random reason. And that is all there is to it. Therefore, proximity to death cannot affect the heart of an atheist. Clearly, therefore, the fear of death itself is the result of some internal change and we call this the voice of *fiṭrah*. Our *fiṭrah* prevails over our hearts when we overcome ignorance and darkness and we are pulled towards belief in God by an indiscernible power. How beautifully the Promised Messiah[as] has said:

آنکھ کے اندھوں کو حائل ہوگئے سو سو حجاب   ورنہ قبلہ تھا ترا رخ کافر و دیندار کا

But for the countless veils covering people's eyes,
Your Countenance should indeed be the goal of every believer and
non-believer.

In short, human *fiṭrah* is strong and undeniable evidence for
the existence of God, which no intelligent person can deny. It is
entirely through His Grace that God sowed a seed of belief in our
fiṭrah for our guidance. The Holy Quran says:

وَفِیۡۤ اَنۡفُسِکُمۡ ؕ اَفَلَا تُبۡصِرُوۡنَ [1]

That is, O people! You do not have to go here and there; Divine
Signs are there in your own selves, if you only pay attention and
try to see.

A poet has said it beautifully:

دل کے آئینہ میں ہے تصویر یار   جب ذرا گردن جھکائی دیکھ لی

In the mirror of my heart I carry the portrait of my Beloved;
If I bow my head but a little, I can see Him.

Regardless of what this poet had in mind, there is no doubt that
God has engraved His image in everyone's heart. But man in his
arrogance is not prepared to bow his head to see Him! God has
placed a spark of His love in every man's *fiṭrah,* but there are few
who make an effort to save it from being extinguished.

---

1. *Sūrah adh-Dhāriyāt,* 51:22.

The Promised Messiah[as] said:

تو نے خود رُوحوں پہ اپنے ہاتھ سے چھڑکا نمک   جس سے ہے شورِ محبت عاشقانِ زار کا

With Your own hands You have sprinkled the mineral of love over souls,

Which has caused agonised cries of pining lovers.

ایک دم بھی کل نہیں پڑتی مجھے تیرے سوا   جاں گھٹی جاتی ہے جیسے دل گھٹے بیمار کا

Not for a moment am I at ease without You;

Life seems to ebb away like the sinking heart of an ailing one.

شور کیسا ہے ترے کوچے میں لے جلدی خبر   خوں نہ ہوجائے کسی دیوانہ مجنوں وار کا

Find out quickly wherefore is this noise in Your street;

Lest someone madly in love perishes.

Argument Based on Creation and the Operational System of the Universe

Now I take up the most renowned of all logical arguments. In fact, this is the only argument upon which the belief of most people is based. As far as the reach of human reason alone is concerned, one cannot think of a more enlightening and impactful argument than this. We should note that we are not discussing the arguments and evidence that descend from heaven and establish the existence of God with utmost certainty, and which not only point towards God but actually make one see Him and reach Him. But rather, here we are referring to the logical arguments that do not lead us beyond the 'ought to be' stage of belief. Of these arguments, the one I would like to present is indeed extremely brilliant. It is due largely to this argument that, despite being totally devoid of the knowledge of God, the world is saved from completely denying His existence. This is the preliminary argument which has always been used in scriptures to awaken the oblivious, and the Holy Quran, too, has used it extensively and repeatedly.

This is the evidence of cause and effect. Academically speaking, it is actually a combination of two arguments. According to one generally well-known argument, the existence of creation as a whole is put forward to prove the existence of a Creator. Due to its simplicity, this argument appeals better to the general masses. According to the other, the study of the universe and its organisation is cited to prove the existence of a Creator, Designer, and Sustainer of the universe. This argument is further divided into several other arguments. For brevity and simplicity, these two arguments will be discussed in a combined form.

The first part of the argument, that creation leads to the existence of a Creator, is very simple in its apparent form. For instance, I am at present staying at a friend's home on Mansuri Hill and writing this treatise. I see many items lying on the table before me, and each one of these teaches me something by its existence. I see paper, a pen, ink, blotting paper, a beautiful paperweight (which prevents papers from flying away). In this room, I have a chair, a table covered with an attractive table cloth to keep the table neat, and some reference books for my use. The mere presence of these things give me the conviction that someone must have made them. Moreover, the room I am in has four walls, a roof, windows, doors, curtains, a rug, and many other objects on the floor. I see these things and I am convinced that they did not come into existence by themselves, but are the fruits of some workman's efforts. If someone tries to convince me that all of these things have come into existence by themselves, I would never believe them; in fact, no one else would be prepared to believe it either. Sadly, however, there are hundreds of thousands of people in this world who would have us believe that this earth, the heavens, animals, vegetation, inanimate objects, heavenly bodies, the earth, and the human body are not created by any Creator but have existed by themselves from eternity. How can I believe them?

I have, before me, a statement by an Arab Bedouin. Someone inquired from him as to what evidence he had for the existence of God. He replied: When someone passing through a jungle sees camel dung, he concludes that a camel must have passed this way; when he sees the footprint of a man in the desert sand, he infers that some wayfarer must have passed this way. Now, looking at this earth, with all its wide tracks, and this heaven, with its sun and the moon and the stars, does it not make one think that these must have a Maker?

What an unpretentious statement that is full of wisdom! Glory be to God! The words of an illiterate Arab Bedouin, the profoundness of which is not understood by the philosophers of Europe and America despite their wisdom and logic!

Concerning the creation and organisation of the universe, the Holy Quran says:

 اَفِی اللّٰهِ شَكٌّ فَاطِرِ السَّمٰوٰتِ وَالْاَرْضِ [1]

---

1. *Sūrah Ibrāhīm*, 14:11.

That is, are you in doubt concerning Allah, Maker of the heavens
and the earth? That God who brought into being the earth and
the heavens from nothingness.

إِنَّ فِى خَلْقِ السَّمٰوٰتِ وَ الْأَرْضِ وَ اخْتِلَافِ الَّيْلِ وَ النَّهَارِ وَ الْفُلْكِ الَّتِى تَجْرِى فِى الْبَحْرِ بِمَا
يَنْفَعُ النَّاسَ وَ مَآ أَنْزَلَ اللهُ مِنَ السَّمَآءِ مِنْ مَّآءٍ فَأَحْيَا بِهِ الْأَرْضَ بَعْدَ مَوْتِهَا وَ بَثَّ فِيهَا
مِنْ كُلِّ دَآبَّةٍ ۚ وَّ تَصْرِيفِ الرِّيٰحِ وَ السَّحَابِ الْمُسَخَّرِ بَيْنَ السَّمَآءِ وَ الْأَرْضِ لَأٰيٰتٍ لِّقَوْمٍ
يَّعْقِلُونَ ¹

Verily, in the creation of the heavens and the earth and in the alter-
nation of night and day, and in the ships that sail in the sea with
that which profits men, and in the water which Allah sends down
from the sky and quickens therewith the earth after its death and
scatters therein all kinds of beasts, and in the change of the winds,
and the clouds pressed into service between the heaven and the
earth are indeed Signs for the people who understand.

وَ فِىٓ أَنْفُسِكُمْ ۚ أَفَلَا تُبْصِرُونَ ²

And also in your own selves there are signs. Will you not then see?

أَفَلَمْ يَنْظُرُوٓا إِلَى السَّمَآءِ فَوْقَهُمْ كَيْفَ بَنَيْنٰهَا وَ زَيَّنّٰهَا وَ مَا لَهَا مِنْ فُرُوجٍ وَ الْأَرْضَ مَدَدْنٰهَا وَ
أَلْقَيْنَا فِيهَا رَوَاسِىَ وَ أَنْبَتْنَا فِيهَا مِنْ كُلِّ زَوْجٍ بَهِيجٍ تَبْصِرَةً وَّ ذِكْرٰى لِكُلِّ عَبْدٍ مُّنِيبٍ ³

Have they not looked at the sky above them, how We have made

1. *Sūrah al-Baqarah*, 2:165.

2. *Sūrah adh-Dhāriyāt*, 51:22.

3. *Sūrah Qāf*, 50:7–9.

it and adorned it with different heavenly bodies, and that there are no flaws in it? We have spread out the earth (despite being round), and placed therein firm mountains; and We have made to grow therein every kind of beautiful species; as a means of enlightenment for those who would ponder and as a reminder to every servant that turns to God.

$$^1 \text{ وَ لِلّٰهِ يَسْجُدُ مَنْ فِي السَّمٰوٰتِ وَالْاَرْضِ طَوْعًا وَّ كَرْهًا}$$

To Allah submits whosoever is in the heavens and the earth [willingly or unwillingly], and cannot overstep the bounds of the law laid down for it by God.

$$^2 \text{ وَ كُلٌّ فِيْ فَلَكٍ يَّسْبَحُوْنَ}$$

All of them float in an orbit, separately without colliding with others.

$$^3 \text{ وَ اِنَّ لَكُمْ فِي الْاَنْعَامِ لَعِبْرَةً نُسْقِيْكُمْ مِّمَّا فِيْ بُطُوْنِهٖ مِنْ بَيْنِ فَرْثٍ وَّ دَمٍ لَّبَنًا خَالِصًا سَآئِغًا لِّلشّٰرِبِيْنَ وَ مِنْ ثَمَرٰتِ النَّخِيْلِ وَالْاَعْنَابِ تَتَّخِذُوْنَ مِنْهُ سَكَرًا وَّ رِزْقًا حَسَنًا اِنَّ فِيْ ذٰلِكَ لَاٰيَةً لِّقَوْمٍ يَّعْقِلُوْنَ وَ اَوْحٰى رَبُّكَ اِلَى النَّحْلِ اَنِ اتَّخِذِيْ مِنَ الْجِبَالِ بُيُوْتًا وَّ مِنَ الشَّجَرِ وَ مِمَّا يَعْرِشُوْنَ ثُمَّ كُلِيْ مِنْ كُلِّ الثَّمَرٰتِ فَاسْلُكِيْ سُبُلَ رَبِّكِ ذُلُلًا يَخْرُجُ مِنْ بُطُوْنِهَا شَرَابٌ مُّخْتَلِفٌ اَلْوَانُهٗ فِيْهِ شِفَآءٌ لِّلنَّاسِ اِنَّ فِيْ ذٰلِكَ لَاٰيَةً لِّقَوْمٍ يَّتَفَكَّرُوْنَ}$$

Look at the milk-producing animals, for in them too there is a

---

1. *Sūrah ar-Raʿd,* 13:16.

2. *Sūrah Yā Sīn,* 36:41.

3. *Sūrah an-Naḥl,* 16:67–70.

lesson for you. We provide you with a drink out of that which is in their bellies; that is, from betwixt the faeces and the blood We provide milk pure and pleasant for those who drink it.

Look at the bee as well. Your Lord directed the bee saying: Make thou houses in the hills and in the trees and in the trellises, and suck the juice of fruits and follow the ways appointed for thee by thy Lord in submission. There comes out of the bellies of the bees honey of various hues, possessing healing qualities for people. Surely in that is a sign for people who reflect.

فَلْيَنْظُرِ الْإِنْسَانُ إِلَى طَعَامِهِ أَنَّا صَبَبْنَا الْمَاءَ صَبًّا ثُمَّ شَقَقْنَا الْأَرْضَ شَقًّا فَأَنْبَتْنَا فِيهَا حَبًّا وَ عِنَبًا وَ قَضْبًا وَ زَيْتُونًا وَ نَخْلًا وَ حَدَائِقَ غُلْبًا وَ فَاكِهَةً وَ أَبًّا مَتَاعًا لَّكُمْ وَ لِأَنْعَامِكُمْ [1]

Now let man look at his daily food. We pour down water from the sky in abundance; then, We cleave the earth a proper cleaving, then We cause to grow therein grain, grapes, vegetables, the olive and the date-palm, walled gardens thickly planted, and fruits and herbage, as provision for you and your cattle.

تَبَارَكَ الَّذِي بِيَدِهِ الْمُلْكُ وَ هُوَ عَلَى كُلِّ شَيْءٍ قَدِيرٌ الَّذِي خَلَقَ الْمَوْتَ وَ الْحَيَوةَ لِيَبْلُوَكُمْ أَيُّكُمْ أَحْسَنُ عَمَلًا وَ هُوَ الْعَزِيزُ الْغَفُورُ الَّذِي خَلَقَ سَبْعَ سَمٰوٰتٍ طِبَاقًا مَا تَرَى فِي خَلْقِ الرَّحْمٰنِ مِنْ تَفٰوُتٍ فَارْجِعِ الْبَصَرَ هَلْ تَرَى مِنْ فُطُورٍ ثُمَّ ارْجِعِ الْبَصَرَ كَرَّتَيْنِ يَنْقَلِبْ إِلَيْكَ الْبَصَرُ خَاسِئًا وَ هُوَ حَسِيرٌ [2]

Blessed is He in whose hand is the kingdom and He has the power over all things, who has created death and life that He might try

---

1. *Sūrah 'Abasa*, 80:25–23.

2. *Sūrah al-Mulk*, 67:2–5.

you—which of you is best in deed; and He is Mighty, the Most Forgiving, who has created seven heavens in harmony. Do you see any flaw in the creation of the Gracious God? Look all around you: Do you see any disparity? Look again, and yet again: thy sight returns to thee frustrated and fatigued.

Do all these things not guide you to God?

قُتِلَ الْإِنْسَانُ مَآ أَكْفَرَهُ ٢
Ruin seize man! How ungrateful he is!

These verses, quoted from different parts of the Holy Quran, point to the existence of God by referring to the creation and organisation of the universe with such unparalleled eloquence that it needs no further explanation. Indeed, for those who wish to ponder, everything in this world points to God. The perception of God gets sharper and more well-defined as one makes progress in knowledge and understanding of the universe and the properties of matter. Take the tiniest particle in the world and contemplate upon it. You will realise that even the most insignificant looking particle operates within a most magnificent and judicious set of laws and it incorporates such arrangement and profound reason that it is simply baffling. The arrangements and purpose of even

---

1. *Sūrah an-Najm,* 53:43.
2. *Sūrah ʿAbasa,* 80:18.

the smallest particles pose an insoluble enigma for the human mind. The Promised Messiah[as] says:

بنا سکتا نہیں اک پاؤں کیڑے کا بشر ہرگز   تو پھر کیونکر بنانا نورِ حق کا اس پہ آساں ہے

Man cannot make even the foot of an insect;
How then can it be easy for him to create the Light of Truth?

Look at a housefly. Even this minor insect is a great miracle of God's magnificent powers. If one spends all his life in researching just the fly and its organs, he will see that his life will come to an end but his research will remain incomplete. Look at the human body itself. Ever since the world was created, hundreds of thousands of the world's best minds, throughout the ages, have occupied themselves with research into its structure and the set of judicious laws that control the function of different human organs, such as the heart and the brain, the kidney, the lungs, the liver, the stomach, the eyes, the ears, the nose, etc. But how much of this God's apparently small treasure have they been able to discover and present to the world? Surely the world will come to an end but the treasures of this miniature universe will not be exhausted.

Take the wild flower that springs up along the edge of your pathway and often gets crushed under the feet of some merciless and unaware wayfarer and disappears permanently from the eyes of the world. In its tiny leaves there are hundreds of veins spread out in the form of a network and each one of these veins is a cosmos in view of its function and system. To acquire the perfect knowledge of this intricate system, even Nūḥ's [Noah] age may not be enough! Cast a glance at the insignificant and scarcely visible seed: hundreds of thousands of which can be held in a fistful, but when sowed in the soil, it grows into a magnificent tree before our eyes and thousands of people may rest under its shade. And have you studied human life? There was a time when man was a part of his father's body in the form of a tiny microscopic sperm, which might not be agreeable for a delicately disposed person to even look at, and then it develops into a handsome and attractive being, who is equipped with the highest faculties of heart and mind.

Let us now look toward the sky. What a scene do the sun, the moon, and the stars present before you. Take the sun: Do you know how far it is from the earth? Its distance from the earth is approximately ninety-three million miles. And let it be no surprise when I say that the sun is one of those stars that is comparatively nearer to the earth. Some of the stars are so far away from the earth that your language does not even specify the numbers to express that distance. Do you know the volume of the sun? Let me inform you of this too. We take pride in the earth's vastness; due to its great vastness it looks flat in spite of being round; it has a diameter of 7,900 miles. By comparison, the sun has a diameter of 865,000 miles. Let it not be surprising when I say that there are many planets in space which are vastly bigger than our sun; there cannot be a comparison between these—not even as much as the robin compares with the eagle.

So much for the physical form of the celestial bodies; but if we study the magnificent system, in accordance with which trillions of these bodies orbit in space, the mind boggles. To top it all, each planet orbits along its own circuit in accordance with its own rules and it is impossible for one to collide with the other or leave its own orbit to enter another. This rule does not apply to the celestial bodies alone; everything on earth is also bound within its own sphere and cannot break free to enter into another. Fire is designed to burn; water to put it out; the tree stands erect at one point on the earth; birds are made to fly in the air; man is designed to walk on the earth and fish to swim in water; the cow is fashioned to eat grass and the lion to feed on other animals. These are a few simple examples; otherwise, everything is bound within its sphere in accordance with its qualities, capabilities, and function, and none has the power to trespass its bounds. Everything serves its particular objective and purpose.

Now contemplate, has this magnificent all-encompassing system of the heavens and the earth come into existence by itself? This judicious and most wise set of laws we see operating on its own in everything—is it without any control by a Higher Being? Are the earth with its innumerable creatures and the heavens with its innumerable celestial bodies their own creators and masters? At this stage, set aside the question, 'If there is a God, who and where is He?' Answer just this: Is your heart content with the notion that this universe and its system exists by itself, without any creator, lord, master, or governor? I am not asking whether you believe in a god or not. My question is only this: Can you honestly declare that the heaven, the earth, animals, vegetation, inanimate matter, celestial bodies, and geological strata came about by mere chance? Is this magnificent system—which has closely knit billions of things in this world into one system— running mechanically without any creator and administrator? I cannot believe that any of the sons of Adam who has a [sensible] heart and mind can be satisfied with the idea that this universe, the compendium of varied wonders, came into existence by itself. To summarise, this universe with its entire judicious and most wise organisation is such strong evidence for the existence of God that no wise person can deny it.

Thus far, I have considered various things and their components in this world individually, and have explained that each thing in itself is such a wonderful entity and operates within such a judicious and most wise system that man is compelled to attribute the creation of the universe to an All-Knowing, All-Powerful, Wise, and All-Governing Being. This conviction becomes even stronger when we study the relationship between different parts of a particular thing or interactions between different things. Let us take the camel, for instance: Suppose we agree that it acquired long legs in accordance with some hidden and unknown law of chance; the question then arises, how did this blind law know that this creature with long legs should also have a long neck, so that its mouth can reach the ground easily. This judicious rule is operational all over the world, not only in camels but in all other animals too; those with long legs have long necks and those with short legs have short necks. It can be argued that this body form has evolved after a long period of adaptation; i.e. because of long legs, necks also lengthened gradually. However, this stance is incorrect as the history of zoology presents no evidence that long-legged animals initially had short necks that grew longer with the passage of time. Moreover, how did the long-legged animals survive when they had short necks? Anyhow, this is a very simple example, but if we ponder, it will become very clear that the different parts of everything have been put together proportionately and appropriately with mind-boggling precision.

Ponder further and we observe an amazing and fascinating spectacle. Can a blind law of nature produce sperm in a man, create a desire in the man and a woman to unite and transfer the sperm into the dark recesses of a woman's womb? Then, this blind law further helps develop one of these sperms into a beautiful child possessing numerous faculties over a period of nine months. Somehow, this blind law then managed to have this baby delivered of the mother's womb. That is to say, all the internal changes in that sperm took place as a chance event. If so, then for God's sake explain to me, how come this blind law could precisely coincide the production of mother's milk with the delivery of the baby, so that the baby's sustenance is ready as the baby arrives in this world. The mother's breasts are not a part of the baby's body. Then how come a mother's breasts started filling up with the milk for the sake of her child. سبحان الله [Holy is Allah!].

$$\text{مَاقَدَرُواالله حَقَّ قَدْرِهِ}^{1}$$

They esteem not Allah with the estimation that is His due.

Furthermore, consider this: the earth came about by itself; the things moving about in it came into existence by themselves; man came into existence from nothing by himself; his nose, ears, and eyes all appeared by themselves. In short, all this happened by chance. Then, how come a magnificent lamp was lit more than ninety million miles away from the earth for the light to facilitate human eyes to see? A tree grew on the earth. It produced seeds, and the seeds were made to fall on the earth and sown

---

1. *Sūrah al-Ḥajj*, 22:75.

therein. However, who determined that water is required for the seeds to sprout, and who arranged for sunlight to fall upon the ocean and carried therefrom billions of tons of water on the winds to the scorched land and caused these clouds to rain? If all of that is brought about by this random force of nature—and that is the force which is the Creator, the Master, the Lord, the All-Knowing, Omnipotent, and Wise Governor, the Guardian that contemplates and considers the appropriateness of circumstances, who arranges for the fulfilment of the needs He causes to arise—we do not care by what name you call it, that is our God and to Him we submit with love and devotion. In short, whichever way we look at this, we cannot but believe that this universe and its judicious and most wise organisation all point to a Being who is the Creator, the Master, the Wise, the All-Knowing, the Omnipotent and the Governor; i.e. He bears all those characteristics that religion attributes to God.

One must remember here that to avoid intellectual jargon and complexities, I have presented the argument in a simple manner so that the young among our dear ones may understand it easily. However, this argument can also be presented in an academic manner. Very briefly, the study of nature reveals that in the innumerable different things in this world, individually or collectively, there exist three things. First, an extremely elaborate and perfect law operates in everything in this world that controls it, as well as its relation to other things. This is termed the Law of Nature. If studied properly, this law constitutes a very strong and clear argument for the existence of a Creator of the universe. Regrettably, some people, out of their short-sightedness, have made this very law a stumbling block for them.

Second, in everything in this world and in this judicious and most wise law [of nature], not only individually but also collectively, there is a definite format and arrangement otherwise known as a design or plan, and no wise person can attribute this to chance.

Third, everything in the world, with its law and design or plan, is working with a definite purpose. That is to say, everything in this universe has a definite purpose. This doctrine, known as teleology, is very compelling evidence for the existence of God. In short, by studying the universe, one is strongly led to the view that it did not come to be by mere chance, but was brought about by the mighty hands of a Conscious and All-Powerful Being.

Belief in God and Western Researchers

Before concluding this discussion, I would like to say something about the Western researchers who are accustomed to studying everything in the light of science and philosophy. Those who deny the existence of God in the West base their conclusion on modern scientific and philosophical ideas. They believe that matter has an inherent quality of transformation and it evolves from a lower to a higher state with the passage of time. They proclaim that this material world has developed as a result of several such transformations, according to the theory of evolution. For instance, they say that man has not always existed in his present form and shape but in ages gone by he was in an extremely primitive state that has gradually evolved to his present form and shape. The same applies to other things in this world; i.e. in their initial state they were lowly and simple but evolved later in accordance with this theory of evolution. Similarly, they claim that most of the things in this world that appear so varied in their sex, form, and features did not vary so much in ages gone by, but the world in its early stages consisted of a few limited and simple things that have evolved gradually into this wondrous universe of today. Thus they argue that the present universe and its elaborate and judicious system cannot be presented as an evidence for an external Creator, for all this has developed naturally as a result of evolution.

Second, Western researchers state that this world has always been operating according to a definitive law and continues to do so, and that with scientific research we can learn the cause of every change and every motion or stillness. They claim that, day by day, they are more fully understanding the law of nature, the properties of matter, and the relationship between various things, and that great progress has been made in various fields of science, such as physics, chemistry, mechanics, anthropology, geology, botany, zoology, anatomy, physiology, astronomy, and psychology. The progress is such that innumerable facts, which earlier were mysteries and completely hidden from our eyes, have been unravelled as manifest realities, and hundreds of false notions, which were established among us as a result of ignorance and established tradition, are disappearing in the light of recent advances in knowledge; and new realities of life and continuance of the universe are being discovered every day. In other words, the things that were previously considered beyond human reason and thus attributed to a Higher Being, in the light of new sciences, can now be established to be the result of some definitive laws of nature. Therefore, to attribute this universe to a Creator, who has not been seen or perceived by anyone, is deemed ignorance.

This is the objection raised by Western research scholars against the existence of God. But if examined carefully, the objection is absolutely absurd. We need not go into detail here, but whether it is wholly or partly correct, the process of evolution does not stand as an argument against the existence of God. Evolution does not shed any light on the genesis of this universe, but refers only to the fact that the things in this world did not always exist in their present form but have evolved from a primitive state. The question is, from where did these primitive types originate? The protagonists of evolution do not shed any definite light on this academically, and unless they do, evolution alone is totally ineffective as evidence for the non-existence of God. Even if it can be proven that man or other things in this world existed in a primitive form initially and have evolved gradually to their present form, does this constitute evidence that this universe does not have a Creator? Certainly not!

One may argue that it has been established that this universe was in a primitive state initially and evolved to a higher and more perfect form as a result of inherent qualities in matter, and that this invalidates the argument given above—i.e. the universe, which is a compendium of innumerable objects, is operating in accordance with an extremely subtle and judicious law and therefore it is under the control of an external Creator and an All-Knowing and Governing Being. This too is a statement born out of ignorance. The existence of such inherent qualities in matter that give it the potential to evolve into a wondrous universe, with parallel development of an extremely judicious law to govern these is in itself a great wonder. If viewed carefully, the initial state of matter as it is described, correctly or incorrectly, is even more wondrous and baffling than the present universe. Obviously the initial state was a seed for the present universe and every wise person can understand that a seed is more wonderful and profound because, although small in size and simple in form, it has all the potential powers, qualities, and perfections hidden in it that subsequently unfold in the tree. Thus, the initial primitive state of this universe proves it to be even more profound and mysterious and constitutes further evidence for the existence of a Creator of this universe. This is because the Creator endowed this initial primitive matter with potential to develop into a magnificent, awe-inspiring, and profound universe, and from it, simultaneously, should come into being supportive and prudent laws of nature, in accordance to which innumerable objects in this universe operate in their corresponding spheres to every one's amazement. Hence, it is naïve to argue against the existence of God on the basis of evolution. In fact, this theory gives even more support to the concept of His profound powers and outstanding creation.

The second objection is that everything in the world, each transformation, each motion, and each stillness is in accordance with a particular law, and, day by day, we are acquiring more and more knowledge about this hidden law of nature, and it is becoming more and more obvious that everything happening in this world is in accordance with some definite law, and that this proves that the law is the only thing and there is no such thing as God. This objection, too, is highly absurd and weak. We have never claimed that the universe is not subservient to any law or a series of causes and is instead governed directly by God without establishing any laws or processes. We agree, nay, we claim and Islam teaches us, that the whole of this universe is subservient to an extremely profound law and intricate processes. Indeed, this law is evidence of the existence of God. So, proving that everything in this universe operates in accordance with a definitive law carries no weight against us. Atheists are unable to adequately answer the question about the origin of this complete and perfect law. Some people would answer that this is an inherent quality of matter, and one law comes into operation as a result of another law, and thus has it been happening and thus will it continue. We ask: From where did this inherent property come? Indeed, one set of laws leads to another, but we will have to believe that this chain of cause and effect, however long, certainly must have a starting point wherefrom it all originated. For instance, scientists assert that it is a law of nature that the earth revolves around the sun. They add further that this law is the result of another law that when two or more forces exert their effect from different directions on something, the latter starts moving in a third direction known as the resultant direction. As the earth is being influenced by forces from different directions, it has started revolving around the sun in a third direction. We agree to that in principle, but our question still stands: From where did these effective forces originate? If it is said that these forces resulted from 'xyz', the question will be: Whence came this 'xyz'? In short, we will have to accept that this universe, and its system, has a starting point incorporating the potential for all the excellences, laws, and properties found in it. Thus, the discussion has now reached the point that has been answered above.

In short, seeking a way to deny the existence of God by

proclaiming intermediary systems and processes is deceitful, and we are not sure how this has come to be accepted by some Western scholars. As far as we are concerned, progress in the knowledge, understanding, and discovery of hidden secrets of the laws of nature only helps to enlighten us and consolidate our belief in God. We realise that this universe, with its extremely judicious laws, is run by a Creator and Master, who is All-Knowing and Wise, and an Omnipotent and Governing Being. If by looking at an ordinary thing we infer that it must have a maker, then looking at this wondrous and judicious universe must greatly strengthen our conviction that this could not possibly have come into existence on its own, but is the clear manifestation of the creative powers of an Omnipotent Higher Being. My dear ones! Think hard. These new sciences and investigations cannot but prove that the law of this universe is far more elaborate and profound than previously thought and that the different objects in this world are governed collectively by a judicious and influential chain of commands. Under these judicious laws, different parts of the universe are not just subservient to their own individual laws, but can influence each other in a wonderful and fascinating manner. Moreover, nothing in this world is useless and superfluous; rather, everything is doing its job, in its own sphere, according to its own law. This 'discovery', if it can be called that, supports us. This does not support any argument against the existence of God. On the contrary, it is a clear manifestation of the great powers of our All-Powerful God.

The truth is that, in principle, this is not a new discovery. The Holy Quran had already given a compendious account of this, fourteen centuries ago, as it said:

أَوَ لَمْ يَرَوْا إِلَى مَا خَلَقَ اللهُ مِنْ شَيْءٍ يَتَفَيَّؤُا ظِلَالُهُ عَنِ الْيَمِينِ وَ الشَّمَآئِلِ سُجَّدًا لِّلّهِ وَ هُمْ دَخِرُونَ وَ لِلّهِ يَسْجُدُ مَا فِي السَّمٰوٰتِ وَمَا فِي الْأَرْضِ [1]

Do people not observe the creation of Allah the Exalted: how everything is affecting its right and left, being subservient to Allah, and everything in the earth and the heavens submits to Divine laws?

وَمَا خَلَقْنَا السَّمَآءَ وَالْأَرْضَ وَمَا بَيْنَهُمَا لَاعِبِينَ [2]

That is, and We created not the heaven and the earth and all that is between the two in sport, without any purpose but with a specific purpose.

The researchers of Europe and America have spent their lifetime aiming to discover these realities, but being blind of faith some of them unfortunately believe that their findings are an attack on religion and the existence of God. The fact of the matter remains that, as knowledge of the universe's perfect organisation and the law of nature is enriched, this simply becomes a clearer indicator of a Wise, All-Knowing, Omnipotent, and Governing Creator, for the discerning. There are a fair number of Western researchers who believe in God, and recent discoveries do not affect their faith; rather, they use it as a tool against atheism. So, my dear ones, do not be afraid of modern knowledge—it is subservient to you. Any progress in modern knowledge can only enhance people's comprehension of the miracles of your God's

1. *Surah an-Naḥl,* 16:49–50.

2. *Surah al-Anbiyāʾ,* 21:17.

Omnipotence. This also establishes with greater certainty that everything in the earth and the heaven is, directly or indirectly, for the benefit of man, as declared in the Holy Quran fourteen centuries ago:

هُوَالَّذِى خَلَقَ لَكُمْ مَّا فِى الْأَرْضِ جَمِيعًا ¹

Whatsoever is in the world, whether in the earth or in the heaven, has been created by Him for your benefit.

وَسَخَّرَ لَكُمْ مَّا فِى السَّمٰوٰتِ وَمَا فِى الْأَرْضِ ²

And Allah the Exalted has subjected all these things to you that you may learn their properties and benefit from them.

Woe be to man! That which his Master had created for his guidance and progress, he has turned it into a cause for his error and ruin.

قُتِلَ الْإِنْسَانُ مَآ أَكْفَرَهُ ³

Ruin seize man! How ungrateful he is!

Surely, this ingratitude can lead man to nowhere except ruin. It should be remembered here that the question of whether or not there is a God is truly beyond the scope of science and the boundaries within which scientists work. Science deals with the

---

1. *Sūrah al-Baqarah*, 2:30.
2. *Sūrah al-Jāthiyah*, 45:14.
3. *Sūrah 'Abasa*, 80:18.

discovery of properties and laws pertaining to matter, and discussion of non-matter or metaphysics is beyond its current scope. Moreover, science does not generally deal with what is not in existence; rather, it deals with what exists, what it is, and the law that governs it. Thus, proving the non-existence of God is beyond the scope of scientific deliberation, at least currently. Of course, the questions as to how did this world begin, what is in this world, how did the world come into existence, how did life start, etc., are within the scope of scientific deliberations. Therefore, scientists can, at most, claim that they have discovered this universe is eternal and that it is governed by a certain set of laws which are automatic and that life started by itself, and on the basis of this research they can conclude academically that there is no God. However, the non-existence of God in itself is not directly within the scope of scientific inquiry.

Moreover, it is also worth remembering that, unfortunately, people have generally fallen into dangerous error in that they do not distinguish between the hypotheses of scientists and established scientific facts. Obviously, scientific declarations can be divided into three types:

First, the hypotheses of scientists

Second, incomplete scientific experiments

Third, established scientific facts

Each of these has a different status and grade, and to attach equivalent significance to all would be a grave error. But the naïve do just that, and regard every statement that emanates from the mouths of scientists and every idea which is expressed by them, including their incomplete experiments or scientific observations, as established facts. Thus, instead of following the truth, because of their ignorance they become blind followers of scientists. Everyone with even an elementary amount of knowledge knows that only those facts can be declared scientifically sound that have proven to be correct through repeated experimentation by multiple scientists over a period of time and continue to be so confirmed, and the underlying reality of which has been validated and also proven academically in a most thorough manner on the basis of general scientific principles by way of cause and effect. Other than that, the views and theories of the scientists or their unfinished experiments can certainly not be called established facts, as they carry the same risk of being erroneous as the statements by other wise and learned people. The truth of the matter is that when some new phenomenon comes to the fore or is discovered based on scientific experiments, it is experimentally studied repeatedly by different people under varying circumstances before it is declared to have arrived at the stage of having been proved true; also, it is studied further and examined in the light of general scientific principles, and if no aspect of it is found to contain any doubt based on such analysis it is only then that it is declared to be a proven and established reality. Before attaining this status, even though some scientific experiments may indeed shed light on the matter, and even though some scientists may have become convinced of its truth, it is nevertheless not designated as an established and accepted reality and truth. Unfortunately, laymen cannot differentiate between the two and accept everything as an established fact. It is yet more outrageous that the hypotheses and theories put forward by scientists on the basis of their research are held as established scientific facts. In other words, three different stages of scientific developments—that are completely distinct from, and unlike each other—are conflated. Thus, science, which is meant to enlighten the human mind with knowledge, ends up doing exactly the opposite: leading one to ignorance and darkness.

Once something is established as a fact on the basis of scientific experiments and observations, it is clear that the academic circles in the world are stirred up and different scientists start positing various ideas and theories in light of the new research; thus, with each new piece of research, new ideas and new theories crop up. The laymen, overawed by the word 'science' or for some other reason, regard all these suggestions as established scientific facts, whereas the real established facts are scarce and the rest are all theories, hypotheses, and ideas of the scientists that not only change every day, but are also disputed among scientists themselves. In short, it is a grave error not to differentiate between scientific hypotheses, incomplete experiments of scientists, and established scientific facts, and to submit slavishly to everything stated or written by any scientist. Unfortunately, this mental and academic slavery has been a characteristic largely of the people of the East, whereas Europeans and Americans usually make a distinction, and accept only those facts as scientific truths that have been confirmed after repeated tests and are also not found lacking in any way when examined on the basis of generally accepted scientific principles.

If we view the topic under discussion according to this principle, we do not see any established scientific fact that can form the basis of any objection to the existence of God. A small proof of this statement is as follows: When some new piece of research is actually confirmed to be an established truth, it becomes an undeniable reality that no scientist can deny. Confirmation requires not only academic certainty but also its practical demonstration by repeated tests under different circumstances in a way that leaves no doubt whatsoever. Obviously, by this stage, no scientist or anyone with a bit of sense can deny it. We observe that, in practice, every established scientific fact is accepted by all scientists, without detraction. Disagreements arise concerning only those matters which have not yet been fully established, or concerning theories put forward by scientists based on their ideas and hypotheses which they have reasoned from established facts.

In short, we observe no disagreement whatsoever regarding established scientific facts. However, with regard to belief in a Higher Being, we observe that many scientists believe in God; in fact, very few of them deny God, and the majority are not deniers. Thus, it is confirmed that there is no established scientific fact from which it can be reasoned with certainty that this universe is operating by itself without any Creator or Master; otherwise, this disagreement among scientists would not exist.

If someone were to ask, what if in the future we have evidence proving that all that exists has come into being on its own and is operating by itself, then what would be the answer? First, such a hypothesis is absurd and childish. But if we must raise such questions, then our answer would be that we seek the truth and would not deny anything that is established as a fact. Whatsoever is proven to be really true and correct cannot be denied by us. Our God told our Messenger[saw] (may my life be sacrificed for him) to say to the Christians: God has no son; nay, ascribing a son to Him is such an utter lie and grave act that the earth and heaven might well nigh reduce to ruin. But despite that, tell them: If a

son of God is confirmed then, ¹أَنَا أَوَّلُ الْعَٰبِدِينَ, meaning that, in this
scenario, I would be the first to worship him. Thirsting for truth
is our second nature, which we have inherited from our beloved
Messenger^saw. So, in principle, our answer would be that we will
believe in whatever is truly established, no matter what that is.
But the reality is that nothing can ever be established that puts
the being of God in doubt, as that would amount to two established facts contradicting each other, and this is clearly impossible. Is it possible, for instance, that, on the one hand, a magnet is
scientifically established to attract iron to itself, and, on the other,
that under similar circumstances it does not? Obviously not. As a
remote possibility, if we did observe this, we will have to reject one
of the two statements; i.e. we would have to believe that one of the
two was not really an established fact but was mistakenly regarded
as such. Therefore, if we were to say hypothetically that scientific
research established that the universe has existed by itself since
eternity and is operating by itself, even then we will not deny God
simply for this reason, because the existence of God is also fundamentally an established scientific fact. There is no reason that, on
the basis of so-called research, we should give up an established
fact, supported by observation since the beginning of creation. In
this circumstance we will have to ponder over how far the new
research put forward is established scientific fact, correct, and
acceptable.

Ponder deeply that scientific facts are accepted because they
are based on logic, common sense, and academic and reasonable arguments based on observation and experiments. When

---

1. *Sūrah az-Zukhruf,* 43:82.

experiment and observation combine with logical argument, this leaves little chance of error (unless the observation is flawed). This, indeed, is the best way of research, and for that reason scientifically established facts are regarded most highly in worldly knowledge. The arguments that establish the existence of God are also based on the same scientific approach. As stated above, the existence of God is established not only by logical arguments but also by experience and observation, like scientific facts. In fact, this experience and observation far exceeds that for scientific facts, both in quantity and quality. Reason can reach only as far as 'there ought to be a God'; only experience and observation can take one further, to the stage of 'God truly exists'. Such experience and observation are bestowed by God Himself so that the capacity of a man to appreciate God is not left incomplete. He says:

$$ \text{لَا تُدْرِكُهُ الْأَبْصَارُ ۖ وَهُوَ يُدْرِكُ الْأَبْصَارَ}^{1} $$

That is, the human eye cannot reach God (i.e. knowledge of God cannot be gained by reasoning alone) but God Himself reaches the human eye.

Meaning God Himself makes such arrangements that enable man to perceive Him, so that his cognizance of God should not remain deficient and wanting. And how exactly does one perceive God? This is a vast question and its detailed answer is given in the second part of this book. Here, it would suffice to indicate briefly that God can be seen by virtue of the words He reveals to His pious servants, which are heavily laden with Divine Signs. This is

---

1. *Sūrah al-Anʿām,* 6:104.

like a good fruit-bearing tree, full of fruit in fruit-bearing season. After tasting the fruit of a fruit-bearing tree in the spring, one can remain in no doubt about the identity of the tree; in the same manner, after tasting the fruit of spirituality, one can identify God as clear as day.

Anyhow, evidence of the existence of God is based, just like scientific facts, on experience and observation (though far more elaborate in its perfection) in addition to logical arguments. Thus, if, for the sake of argument, some scientific research emerges that appears to contradict the existence of God, even then we would not reject the existence of God, but would rather examine this new research to determine to what degree it is correct and acceptable. We believe that a detailed assessment will only lead to the conclusion that God does exist. The scientific evidence that appears to contradict the presence of God is either misunderstood or based on flawed observation.

The existence of God, as it will be proved later, is established by such complete and perfect observation that to suggest that any real scientific research can oppose it is putting two truths in contradiction to one another, which is impossible. If science attacks our observation, it will be laying the axe on its own root, because its own basis is observation. Anyway, this is a superfluous and premature question; what happens in the future will be dealt with in the future. There is absolutely no doubt that, up till now, there is no established scientific fact which can be presented against the existence of God in a logically valid manner. The everlasting truth is that this universe, with all its innumerable, varied, and wondrous objects, and extremely judicious law operating in all things, and an amazing organisation, has brought together its innumerable objects of divergent nature into a single string. Because of this, innumerable natural mechanisms are in operation at a distance of thousands or millions of miles to provide for the needs of the tiniest of objects in this world; this indeed constitutes strong evidence to support the fact that this universe is ruled by a Wise, All-Knowing, Omnipotent, and a Governing Being whose dominion encompasses everything.

Why do Modern Philosophical Concepts Cause People to Stumble?

Before concluding this discussion, I would like to explain briefly why, despite the fact that modern European philosophy or the hypotheses of some scientists (irrespective of being right or wrong or the extent to which they are right or wrong) cannot really be grounds for objections to the existence of God, many people in this age are stumbling due to them. Modern European theories have misled people because of two reasons. First, Western researchers posited the idea that matter has an inherent property to transform and evolve from a lower to a higher form and that everything in this world, particularly man, was the miracle of this evolution. Devoid of any spiritual insight concerning God, as they were, suspicions thus arose in their minds about the existence of a God ruling over the world, and they began to think that this world came into being by itself and was moving along and operating as a result of the inherent qualities of matter. Thus, they finally came to believe in this very notion; i.e. that the universe was operating like a machine and all the transformations and the panorama was the result of this internal mechanism, and so on.

This doubt has already been dealt with above. If observed carefully, the nature of industrial law operating in the world itself demands that we believe in a Higher Being, who is distinct and has placed in matter such judicious and most wise laws; and then, matter itself, with all its states and properties, demands a Creator and Master as well. It has also been pointed out that, besides the mechanism, there is also a definite design and purpose (i.e. teleology) in the world. All of this points to an independent Intelligent Designer who is the Creator and Master with a decretive will. This will be elaborated upon later in this book.

Second, modern European philosophy has become a stumbling block for some people, as the theory of evolution has presented the creation of the universe and especially of man in a way that appears contradictory to the formal teachings of the known revealed religions of this age. It is but natural that when the credibility of a revealed religion is called into question by a particular argument and one is unable to defend or counter that argument, then one can develop doubts concerning the existence of God. He starts thinking that what was attributed to God turned out to be incorrect, therefore, all this religious business is false and God too is nothing but a figment of imagination. The people in this age face exactly the same situation vis-à-vis the theory of evolution. The Christians from their priests, the Muslims from their *maulavīs,* the Hindus from their *pundits,* and others from their religious scholars used to hear that in the beginning it was all smoke or water from which God created all these diverse things, and that God created the heaven, the earth, and all that is between them in six 24-hour days and then he made a body out of clay and breathed into it and thus Adam was created and out came Eve from his rib and the progeny of the two started to flourish, and the human race has existed for seven thousand years. According to some, matter, under Divine direction, assumed the form of an egg, which split into two parts, one of which developed into the earth and the other into heaven, and that man and woman emerged from God, or that God perspired and the universe was created from the drops of His sweat, and so on. With this background understanding of creation, recounted by their clergy, *maulavis,* or *pundits,* when people came to appreciate that scientific research had proven all of these stories to be inaccurate—and they also learned that the process of evolution is the basis of the development of this wonderful universe, and the existence of humans is the culmination of the process of evolution over millions of years where lower forms of life evolved into higher forms—this made people disillusioned with religion. They became overwhelmed by new scientific discoveries and renounced their faith in God.

The greatest responsibility for this outrageous insult to religion lies with the Christian priests in the West. Being first to hear about newer philosophical and scientific concepts, the clergy reacted in such a manner that exposed the weakness of their religious concepts to all; disillusioned with the response of the clerics and incapable to counter these arguments for themselves, thousands of people turned to atheism. Aware of the defeat of the clergy against science, other religious nations also found themselves unable to present counterarguments to these concepts, paving the way for one defeat after another. Had the people reflected a little, this indeed was a very simple matter. First, many of the

beliefs about the creation of the earth and humanity found prevalent among the followers of different religions today are in fact
the commentaries and interpretations of later scholars, and not
based on their revealed Scriptures or other authentic texts of
these religions. This being the case, such interpretations being
proven wrong does not in any way justify the religion to be criti-
cized. Second, some concepts about the creation of the universe
became part of religious books because of certain later alterations
and mistranslations and were never mentioned in a revealed Book
in the first place. Therefore, blaming the teachings of religion is
clearly unjustified. Third, some of these ideas are indeed found in
revealed Books but have been misunderstood by most people and
this misinterpretation has provided modern researchers with the
opportunity to criticise.

For instance, it is stated in the Holy Quran that God created
the earth and the heaven in six *ayyām*. Some people have erred
in translating it as 24-hour days, whereas the Arabic word '*yaum*',
although meaning 'a day', often means just a period of time or a
particular era; pre-Islamic Arab poets frequently used the word
'*yaum*' in this sense. However, some people, because of their
naivety or lack of knowledge, translated it to 'six days' and thence
some took it to mean 24-hour days, despite the fact that the context of the verse clearly suggests that the word 'day' is not used
here to refer to the commonly known day of twenty-four hours.
The concept of day as we know relates to the rotation of the earth
and its orbit in relation to the sun, whereas the verse refers to the
time before the creation of the sun and the earth. God says: We
created the earth and the heaven, the sun, the moon, and the stars
in 'six days'. Inevitably, the day herein means the day before the

creation of solar days—i.e. an age, epoch, or time. Thus, not only the Arabic lexicon but also the context of the verse proves that '*yaum*' here does not mean the commonly known day, but an age, epoch, or time. Accordingly, the Quranic verse would mean: We created the universe in six different periods, stage by stage. This is in complete concordance with the scientific point of view, as the scientists believe that this universe evolved to its present condition gradually through several stages and periods.

Likewise, for instance, one hadith states that this world is seven thousand years old and that Adam was created five thousand years before the Holy Prophet, peace and blessings of Allah be on him. Some people wrongly inferred that the human race started only a few thousand years ago, giving the advocates of evolution an opportunity to criticise. The fact is that Islam never claimed that this universe has existed for only a few thousand years and that there was nothing before; to attribute this notion to Islam is absolute ignorance and naivety. According to Islamic doctrine, no Divine attribute is permanently non-functional in any age and each attribute manifests itself in one way or another during all ages. As creation is one of the Divine attributes, it would be absolutely un-Islamic to believe that creation started only five to seven thousand years ago and there was nothing before that. It is certain from this that the above-mentioned hadith cannot imply that the world is only a few thousand years old, but rather, is as the Muslim divines have written, and the reformer of this age and Founder of the Ahmadiyya Movement, the Promised Messiah, may peace be upon him, has elaborated.[1]

---

1. See *al-Ḥakam,* 30 May 1908; *Chashma-e-Maʿrifat,* p. 160.

That is to say, this hadith means that the world has passed through several cycles and the present cycle of the human race commenced several thousand years ago; we are unsure how many similar cycles the earth has passed through. A famous Islamic scholar and Sufi, Ḥaḍrat Muhyiddin ibn-e-Arabi[rta], writes that once in a vision he was shown that there had been hundreds of thousands of Ādams in this world and when a cycle of one Ādam came to an end that of the next started. Only God knows how many cycles this world has gone through.[1] Therefore, by correctly understanding the meaning of the hadith, there remains no room for any objection. The notion that there was no creation of God on this earth a few thousand years ago and God forbid, God was sitting idle is utterly contrary to the teachings of Islam.

Likewise, the Holy Quran says: We made Ādam of clay and then put life into him. Some people have inferred that God made a dummy out of clay and breathed life into it and in this way the human race commenced. But the Quranic verse implies only that there are earthly elements in Ādam's make-up, which is why he inclines easily to material things; that is why God infused an element of spirituality into the nature of human beings, so that his earthly elements do not hinder his spiritual progress. In other words, a very subtle matter, which the Holy Quran characteristically stated in metaphorical language, has been taken in its material sense and thus made the target of criticism. However, even if the verse is taken in the literal sense, I maintain that this verse cannot be faulted in any way. This is because the primary purpose of the revelation of the Holy Quran is to bring about spiritual

---

1. See *Futūḥāt-e-Makkiyyah,* ch. Ḥudūthud-dunyā, vol. 3.

and moral reformation of the world; to describe the details of the creation of the universe is not the main reason for the revelation of this Holy Book. If required to meet the purpose of its revelation, the Holy Quran mentions certain subjects to a point and no more. For example, it is not the aim of the Holy Quran to explain the details of medical science, because the Holy Quran is not a book of medicine. However, as the health of a person does have an impact on his morals and spirituality, Islamic Shariah touches upon some key tenets of human health that are necessary for safeguarding one's health. The information given in the Holy Quran about health, however, is limited to that which is needed to meet the real purpose of its revelation. If the above-mentioned Quranic verse is interpreted in the light of this principle, then surely it cannot be faulted. The Holy Quran simply states that God created man from ringing clay wrought from mud and then ordained life into him.[1] This means that man is a rational animal who has been created quite distinctly from other animals to make progress with his faculty of reasoning. Second, his body and soul are both created by God in a particular manner. However, the Holy Quran does not specify the type of clay, as all chemical salts are a part of clay. It also does not mention how God created man from clay, over how long a period, and through how many stages, and how many types of stages he was made to pass in order to reach his present state, and so on. Likewise, when God put life into man, whence and how was that done; through how many stages, and types of stages was it inserted in, and how did its development take place? The Quran considered these details as irrelevant to its

---

1. *Sūrah al-Ḥijr*, 15:34.

purpose and, thus, made no mention of these. Therefore, no scientist can find fault with the Holy Quran as it describes the creation of man concisely and fittingly, which does not conflict with any established scientific facts, but serves as a beacon of light for science on fundamentals. If someone adds his own comments on this Quranic statement and his comments conflict with science, then he is responsible for it—Islam cannot be criticised for that.

Likewise, a hadith states that Eve was created from Adam's rib. From this some have understood that Adam's body was slit and Eve was created from his rib bone, giving an opportunity to scientists to criticise, whereas, as is characteristic of revealed Books, these words have been used metaphorically. The hadith implies that the woman has been created to be in the company of man and she is an inevitable part of man's life and his life companion. However, the man must keep in mind that, just as the rib is curved, for certain beneficial reasons, the woman has been created with some inherent frailties; therefore, a man should keep these frailties in mind and treat her with courtesy and understanding. The Holy Prophet, peace and blessings of Allah be on him, has used precisely the same words in another hadith: woman is like a curved rib and that is the beauty of the fair sex; therefore, men should be mindful of woman's inherent frailty and try not to straighten it to the extent that it breaks and loses the beauty of its gender.

In short, after a careful study of the words used in the Holy Quran or authentic hadith with reference to the creation of the universe or creation of man, these cannot be criticised at all. Those who have criticised them or considered them objectionable, do so because of their own ignorance or lack of understanding.

Likewise, I believe, those teachings of other revealed books that have been considered objectionable have been mostly misread and misunderstood. Their true meanings have not been understood. If there is anything objectionable, it is certainly the result of subsequent amendments; unfortunately, none of the revealed Books has escaped this with the exception of the Holy Quran. Even the staunchest adversaries admit that the Holy Quran is preserved in its original revealed form; therefore, we claim that no justifiable objection can be sustained against the statements of the Holy Quran. No scientific fact contradicts any of the Quranic teachings. This is impossible also because the Holy Quran is the Word of God, and nature—science being a description of nature—is the act of God. There cannot be any contradiction between the words and acts of God.

Before concluding this discussion, it is particularly necessary to add that the notorious theory of Darwin is up till today merely a theory and not an established scientific fact, and many scientists have forcefully rejected it. The obituary of a world renowned scientist, Sir John Ambrose Fleming, which was published in newspapers, mentions that while Sir John was a very renowned scientist, he did not deny miracles and regarded Darwin's theory of evolution as a mere figment of imagination.[1]

Therefore, raising objections about the existence of God on the basis of this theory cannot be considered reasonable.

---

1. *Civil and Military Gazette,* Lahore, 22 April 1945.

God is Uncreated

Before proceeding to the next argument, it is necessary to dispel one doubt that arises in the minds of some naïve people—particularly the young—and that is, if God created this universe, then who created God? That is to say, if it is pertinent to ask who is the Creator and Master of this world, then it should also be pertinent to ask who is the Creator and Master of God? The answer is—regardless of the fact that such a question cannot arise vis-à-vis God, as it will be established later—even if we suppose that the Being who is the Creator and Master of this universe has been created by another being, it does no harm to the argument, for in that case, we will call the higher being God and consider the lower being as one of the creation, as one cause out of the chain of causes, and as one of the intermediate links in the creation. If someone asks who is the creator and master of that higher being, the answer is that if that higher being is the creation of a still higher being, then the highest being will be called God and each of the lower beings will be considered one of the creation. In short, whoever will mark the end-point of this chain; i.e. whoever is considered as the first link of this chain, with no one higher, Him shall we call God and all else His creation.

If someone thinks that the question of who is the Creator and Master of a particular being arises on and on ad infinitum about every being, and so, no such being would be established that could be called the first being, the answer is that such an eventuality would be logically impossible. If we accept no one as the first being in this chain, inevitably we will have to deny the existence of all the lower beings, including this universe, which resulted from the first being. In other words, the universe, and everything in it, is nothing but imagination and in reality there is no earth, no heaven, no moon, no sun, no stars, no human beings, no animals, no trees, no water, no air, and nothing else. For instance, let us call this universe 'A', and call its Creator 'B', and suppose 'C' created 'B', and 'D' created 'C', and go on suggesting that every being is created by another higher being ad infinitum. We will never be able to establish a cause that can be called the first cause, and when the first cause cannot be established, none of the subsequent causes would be established; i.e. a failure to establish the first cause will render all subsequent causes void. Reverting to the example above, if 'D' is not established, inevitably 'C' would not be established; if there is no 'C', there would be no 'B', and if there is no 'B' then there would no 'A'. Thus denying 'D' inevitably leads to denial of 'A', whereas existence of 'A' (the letter we have assigned to this world) is unanimously accepted—no one can deny that. Therefore, the kind of reasoning that fails to establish the first cause is faulty, because that leads you to deny the existence of the universe. Therefore, we are obliged to determine a first cause; i.e. to believe in a Being above whom there is no being and obviously that can be the only one who is uncreated, and we call Him God. To summarise, however prolonged this chain [of cause and effect] may be, we will have to determine its end point; i.e. we will have to accept some being at the origin of this chain and that first being is God, who is uncreated, and all others below Him—be they superior and more eminent than each other in their natural and inherent capabilities—are without exception part of creation and governed by the One God.

Now I would like to briefly state that the question, 'Who

is the creator or master of God', is in fact wrong because such a question about God should not arise. The concepts of Divinity and being created are mutually exclusive; it is logically impossible to combine the two. The term 'God' has to be reserved for the One highest of all, and the term creation infers the existence of a Higher Being who has the capacity to create. Therefore, these two concepts cannot be combined in any way. Calling someone 'created' implies that we believe in the existence of some higher being, who is its creator and master. Thus, if 'God' is created, inevitably there should be a being above 'God' who is the creator of 'God', master of 'God', sovereign over 'God', and one who sustains 'God'; in short, one who is above and superior to 'God' in every respect. If there is truly such a being then that higher being is God, not the so-called subordinate 'God' who is created and possessed and governed. No wise man can use the word God for the subordinate being in the presence of the higher being. Think and think again: you can call a being God only as long as you regard Him as uncreated. As soon as you introduce the concept of him being created, you are compelled to accept the existence of a superior being above him, who should be the creator and master of the former. This immediately transfers the status of God from the subordinate to the superior. In short, the being who is determined to be created cannot be God; the being who is his creator and superior will be called God. So it is established that one being cannot be both God and the creation. It is impossible for a being to be God as well as created, and so, if we accept a being as God, then the question of His creator is totally irrational.

Third, I would like to respond to this doubt, though it is absolutely beyond question. Let us suppose for a moment that God is created and then see the outcome. Obviously, everything has some characteristics and properties which distinguish it from other things. For instance, water has properties not found in air and stone, and that is how we distinguish it from air and stone. If those properties are taken away from water then it no longer remains water. In short, everything has some characteristics and properties that characterise its existence and distinguish it from other things. When we use the word God about one being, our reason suggests some attributes that would make Him worthy of the title, and distinguish Him from other beings; i.e. these attributes are pillars of being Divine, and if stripped of them He would no longer be God. For instance, reason counsels us that if God exists, He should be eternal and immortal; i.e. He should be everlasting. Logic suggests that if there is a God, He should be self-subsisting; i.e. He should be able to sustain Himself without any support from any other being. He should be omnipotent; i.e. His authority should be absolute and no one should be able to interfere with His works. And He should be one; i.e. He should be one and unique with no one else to claim equality with Him. Reason tells us that if there is a God, He should be permanent and independent in His attributes and the existence of His attributes should not depend on the will of any other being.

Thus, whoever we can call God must have some of the attributes I have explained above, because without these attributes, the perpetual system of the universe cannot be sustained. That is, these attributes and the like are pillars for the Divine Throne, without which it [the universe] cannot exist. If we assume that God is created, then He cannot possibly have any of these attributes. For instance, if God is created, He cannot be eternal and we will have to believe that He is recent. A created God cannot be immortal and we will have to believe that He is mortal. If God is created, He cannot be self-subsisting and He would have to be sustained by one who is His creator and master. If God is created, He cannot be omnipotent and we will have to believe that His powers are limited and that the one who is his creator and master can interfere with His works as and when he likes. If God is created, He cannot be one and we will have to consider the possibility of many other gods besides Him, since there is no reason why the being that could create one god would not have created many gods to affirm the vastness of his attributes of creation, power, and sovereignty. If God is created, He cannot be permanent and independent in any of His attributes and we will have to believe that each of His attributes is dependent on the will and mercy of one who created Him, because each attribute of the one who is created is also created and governed by the Creator. In short, as a consequence of believing that God is created, all His attributes—arguably the pillars of Divine Throne—become invalid and God appears like ordinary created beings that seek support from their creator and master in everything and have no independent existence at all.

In short, from whichever angle you look at it, to be God and to be created are so opposed and contradictory to each other that they cannot exist together in one being in any way. Therefore, we are compelled not to deem the Being we call God to be created and not to use the name 'God' for the one we deem to be created.

Why Not Consider this Universe Itself to be Uncreated?

After this, I would like to dispel another doubt that arises in the minds of most, and is generally presented by European atheists: If we have to ascertain that God is uncreated and believe that He is Self-Existent and Eternal and without any creator and master, why not bring an end to all of the debates by declaring that this universe is self-existent and uncreated? This is a doubt that can and does arise in the minds of most, and is generally presented by atheists. If pondered carefully, this question is obviously based on lack of deliberation, a conjecture of the naïve, and largely baseless. This doubt is based on the notion that because God is believed to be uncreated, it is therefore also possible for anything to come into existence by itself without the agency of a creator. With this established, there is no reason for us to regard this universe as created and believe in the existence of a God over it; why not pronounce the universe as uncreated and self-existent and call it a day. The answer is: We regard the universe created not because it is a must for everything to be created, but because its properties prove it to have been created. If we had advanced the principle that without exception everything must be created, regardless of its properties, then this criticism—that either consider God to also be a created being, or abandon this principle and accept the possibility that the universe could be uncreated—could have been levelled against us. So this point, that because we are obliged to believe in God's uncreatedness there is no harm in regarding the universe as uncreated, is invalid. Everything has its own specific properties and one can only form an opinion about them accordingly. The properties of water are different from those of fire and stone and air. It will be naïve for us to regard them under same rules and assess them in the same manner. We cannot form an opinion about God by using the criteria applicable to worldly objects; and we cannot explore the universe using criteria applicable to God. Everything will be judged individually by criteria according to its specific features.

When we apply this principle, it becomes obvious that God is not created but the universe certainly is. We have established in our discussion above that He cannot be created because if we accept Him as such; i.e. admit a creator for Him, Godhood shifts from Him to His creator instantaneously. In other words, as soon as the idea of createdness crosses our mind, God remains God no more. Second, if we believe that God is created, we have to deny all those attributes that are arguably the pillars upon which the Divine Throne rests, without which God remains God no more. In short, it has been established beyond doubt that God cannot be created. The case of the universe has also been discussed above in detail, that its properties prove it to have been created. Had it been otherwise, we would readily accept its uncreatedness. Whereas God, on account of His attributes, convinces us that He was not created, the condition of the universe bears witness that it is a manifestation of the creative power of some Higher Being and is sustained by Him.

First, we do not have to refute fundamental characteristics of any part of the universe by believing it be to be created. But if we believe God to be created, then we have to deny all of His fundamental attributes, vide supra. For instance, if we believe water, fire, and air to be created, we do not have to deny any of their natural particulars; if we believe that man is created, it does no harm to his status as man; if we believe that the earth, the moon, and the sun are created, it has no impact on their fundamental characteristics. Likewise, if we ascribe createdness to other elements, their nature remains unaltered. In short, none of the basic features of anything in this world, high or low, compound or single, is invalidated by assuming that it is created; all of them remain intact as they are. However, if we assume that God is created, all of His attributes that form the pillars of His Divinity are invalidated and He no longer remains God. So it is unwise to suppose that because we believe that God is uncreated, there would be no harm in believing that the universe is uncreated. Water, being a liquid, acquires the shape of the vessel it is poured in, but no wise man can suggest that a stone would do the same. It is all sheer ignorance that cannot engage the attention of any sensible person. God is uncreated because He could not be otherwise; i.e. it is impossible for Him to be created because that would invalidate His Godhood (just as it is impossible for stone to assume the shape of the vessel it is put in, because in that case it would no longer remain a stone), whereas being created does not conflict with any of the basic properties of anything else in the world. The difference is clear.

So far, I have only stated that by assuming createdness of anything in this world, we are not compelled into denying any of its properties, therefore we should believe that it is created. That is the general principle which establishes the fact that this universe is created. Now, I would like to state briefly that not only is there no reason to deny the createdness of this universe, but also the state of this universe compels us to declare that it is created.

First, there is plurality in the universe. The universe is not one thing; it is a collection of innumerable things. This magnificent plurality, which is beyond man's comprehension, demands that there ought to be a Creator and Master of this universe who can hold this multitude together within a single organisation. By contrast, God is believed to be one and unique, both by religion and by reason, and therefore needs no organiser.

Second, there is variety in the universe; i.e. it is not a collection of one type of thing, but consists of innumerable things of distinct forms and types, each with its individual characteristics, orbiting in its own sphere and operating under separate laws. This variety also establishes the need for a Creator, Master, Omnipotent, and Organising Being who can align all of these innumerable variants operating under different laws on the string of a collective law. As for God, He is One, so there is no question of variety.

Third, everything in this universe is subject to decline and change; i.e. nothing in this universe stays in one condition, but it is changing and decreasing its limited age all the time. That also proves that this universe does not exist on its own but is under the governance of a Higher Being. However, God is unchanging and unaffected by time and that is how it should be.

Fourth, everything in the universe has a limit in terms of its capacity, natural tendencies, and sphere of action. Nothing in this world has even one attribute that is so perfect that it has no limitations or restrictions. This limitation of attributes and qualities is indicative of a Being who determines these limits; i.e. there exists a Being who has set boundaries and limitations on everything in this universe according to a law and who Himself is independent of all limitations.

Fifth, nothing in the universe is self-sustaining, but rather, depends on others for its survival. Modern scientific research has demonstrated that everything in this universe impacts other things and is impacted by other things, which is required for its survival. In other words, nothing in this world can exist by itself. This very fact alludes to the verity that this universe cannot exist by itself and is sustained by a Higher Being who has judiciously organised and set everything in its appropriate place in this world.

Sixth, there is a design or arrangement in this universe which demands a Conscious Designer; that is not the case as far as God is concerned.

Seventh, the universe appears to be working to a purpose and a final cause; under a definitive plan, the underlying lifespan of everything, as evidenced by a study of nature, demands another being in the background pulling the invisible strings of the universe and leading it to a specific purpose and end. By contrast, the question of final cause vis-à-vis God does not arise, for He is the One and the Only, the First and the Last (or Alpha and Omega), Self-Sustaining and Independent, and comprehending all excellences. Similarly, all other conditions and particulars of the universe prove its createdness.

In short, the state of this universe compels us to declare that it is created and owned (by a master). By contrast, the attributes of God do not demand being created; Divinity and creations are mutually exclusive connotations and cannot coexist in one being. This question—i.e. if God can be uncreated why then cannot the universe be the same—arises out of naivety and ignorance. The fact is that everything is created except God, who has no creator. Everything is governed except God, who has no governor, and everything is owned except God, who has no master. God is the focal point at which all lines converge and there is no way beyond. Blessed is he who understands this and escapes annihilation.

The Holy Prophet^{saw} is reported to have said: You can go on asking about everything as to who created it, but when you reach God, ask no more. A naïve person may think that he closed the door to independent research for his followers and prohibited them from asking this academic question to save them from doubts. But the Holy Prophet^{saw} only meant what has been stated above; i.e. the question of being created can arise about everything except God; anyone raising that question about God proves his ignorance. The Holy Prophet^{saw} did not close the door on knowledge but on ignorance. He did not block the way to research but forbade pursuing superstition. اللّهم صلّ عليه وسلّم ويا ايّها الّذين أمنوا صلّوا عليه وسلّموا تسليماً [O Allah, bless Muhammad and prosper him; O ye who believe, you should also invoke blessings on him and salute him with the salutation of peace].

To summarise, this vast universe—with an extremely judicious organisation that appears to be operating, individually and collectively, in multitude of its distinctly shaped, ever-changing, non-self-existent and limited objects—bears witness to the fact that it is not by itself but has come into existence through the agency of the creative powers of a Higher Being and is sustained and maintained by the same Higher Being, who Himself is uncreated and is without a master. He is the last cause and to Him all else converges. I end this discussion on a very elegant poem by the Promised Messiah^{as}:

کس قدر ظاہر ہے نُور اس مبدءِ الانوار کا ۔۔۔ بن رہا ہے سارا عالَم آئینہ ابصار کا

How manifest is the light of the Source of all light,

  Turning the Universe into a mirror for eyes to see His reflection.

چاند کو کل دیکھ کر میں سخت بیکل ہوگیا ۔۔۔ کیونکہ کچھ کچھ تھا نشاں اس میں جمالِ یار کا

When I saw the moon yesternight I was overwhelmed with longing,

  For it reminded me a little of the beauty of my Beloved Lord.

اس بہارِ حسن کا دل میں ہمارے جوش ہے ۔۔۔ مت کرو کچھ ذکر ہم سے ترک یا تاتار کا

His eternal beauty has set our hearts afire;

  Mention not to us the beauty of the Turk or Tartar.

ہے عجب جلوہ تری قدرت کا پیارے ہر طرف ۔۔۔ جس طرف دیکھیں وہی راہ ہے ترے دیدار کا

O Beloved! Present, strange and wonderful, is the spectacle of Your glory all around;

  Whichever way we turn is the path that leads to You.

چشمۂ خورشید میں موجیں تری مشہود ہیں ۔۔۔ ہر ستارے میں تماشہ ہے تری چمکار کا

Your own light burns bright in the resplendent fountain of the sun;

  In every star can be seen the spectacle of Your glowing beauty.

تُونے خود زخموں پہ اپنے ہاتھ سے چھڑکا نمک ۔۔۔ اس سے ہے شورِ محبّت عاشقانِ زار کا

With Your own hands have You sprinkled salt upon the souls,

  Causing a great commotion of love among Your anguished lovers.

کیا عجب تو نے ہر اِک ذرّہ میں رکھے ہیں خواص   کون پڑھ سکتا ہے سارا دفتر اِن اسرار کا

You have invested each particle with amazing qualities;
  Who can ever decipher Your boundless mysteries?

تیری قدرت کا کوئی بھی انتہا پاتا نہیں   کس سے کُھل سکتا ہے بیچ اس عقدۂ دشوار کا

No one can fathom the extent of Your limitless power;
  Nor can anyone unravel the mysteries of this intricate knot.

خُوب رُویوں میں ملاحت ہے ترے اس حُسن کی   ہر گل و گلشن میں ہے رنگ اس تری گلزار کا

It is Your beauty that lends charm to every beautiful face;
  So are the hues and colours of each flower and garden but a reflec-
  tion of Your loveliness.

چشمِ مست ہر حسیں ہر دم دکھاتی ہے تُجھے   ہاتھ ہے تیری طرف ہر گیسوئے خمدار کا

The love-laden glances of a beautiful face ever remind us of You;
  Every curly lock points its finger in Your direction.

آنکھ کے اندھوں کو حائل ہوگئے سو سو حجاب   ورنہ قبلہ تھا ترا رُخ کافر و دیں دار کا

To every believer and non-believer, Your countenance alone
should be the focal point;
  But alas! The sightless suffer from a thousand veils.

ہیں تری پیاری نگاہیں دلبرا اِک تیغِ تیز   جس سے کٹ جاتا ہے سب جھگڑا غمِ اغیار کا

O my Beloved, Your enchanting glances are like the sharp sword
  Which cuts off all bondages of loyalty and love for others.

تیرے ملنے کے لئے ہم مل گئے ہیں خاک میں   تا مگر درماں ہو کچھ اس ہجر کے آزار کا

Only to win Your love have I reduced myself to dust;
  Hoping, the pangs of separation may thus be assuaged a little.

ایک دم بھی کل نہیں پڑتی مجھے تیرے سوا   جاں گھٹی جاتی ہے جیسے دل گھٹے بیمار کا

Except when I am with You I am ever restless;
  Like the sinking heart of a patient, life seems to be ebbing away.

شور کیسا ہے ترے کوچے میں لے جلدی خبر   خوں نہ ہو جائے کسی دیوانہ مجنوں وار کا

Wherefore this noise in Your neighbourhood? Pray, tarry not!
  Lest some love-lorn lover should perish unknown.

Knowledge of Good and Evil as an Argument

The next logical argument for the existence of God that I would like to present relates to the moral code inscribed in the *fiṭrah* [nature] of every man. In other words, just as the last argument related to the physical law that appears to be operating individually and collectively in human beings and other things in the universe, this argument is based on the moral code that is operating in the *fiṭrah* of all human beings and no wise person can deny this. The knowledge of good and evil is inscribed in the *fiṭrah* of man and no one is devoid of it. It is possible, indeed, that it may be weakened or suppressed almost to the point of extinction in someone as a result of external influences; even then it cannot but show up somehow, in one form or another, from time to time. Everyone, however wretched his condition may be, by nature, likes good and hates evil. An extremely callous, long-standing, and habitual thief, who has been burying his *fiṭrah* in the dark veils of sin with repeated acts of stealing and snatching other peoples' belongings illegally, jaded by chiding from people or to protect himself from the probing of his own conscience, may shamelessly justify himself saying that his act of stealing is not a bad act because, like other people who undertake various professions to earn their livelihood, he too is working hard, toiling and risking his life to sustain his family. Despite all this, he certainly passes through times when his conscience reproaches him and tells him that his deeds are improper and malicious. That is why, many a time, when a thief grows old and realises that the end is nigh, he becomes inclined to give up thieving and starts paying attention to making amends with his conscience. Even if someone's conscience is utterly muted, so much so that he starts taking pride in his misdeeds and apparently has lost the sense of good and evil completely, it will not be hidden from careful observers that in fact such a person is not devoid of the natural virtue called the sense of good and evil. In dealing with others he appears to have no conscience but when it comes to others dealing with him his suppressed conscience wakes up and he would never agree to give up the smallest of his rights, as determined by his sense of good and evil. For instance, take a long-standing and habitual thief who has annihilated his *fiṭrah* by repeated acts of stealing and may feel or appear to feel justified in that—but when someone else lays his hands on his belongings, his half-dead *fiṭrah* comes alive to stand guard over his rights. Similarly, an adulterer, who is always on the lookout to violate the chastity of the daughters, sisters, and wives of others, and indulges in his profane act so much that if someone attempts to stop him, he would shamelessly defend himself saying that there was nothing wrong with it, as he did so with the consent of the other party and that in any case others should mind their own business. But if someone else lays their hands on his own family, he goes mad with rage and he forgets that if he is entitled to fulfil his sensual desires, so are others. Likewise, a habitual liar may gain pleasure by deceiving others, but when someone else deceives him by lying, he becomes filled with rage and anger and seeks revenge.

In short, the knowledge of good and evil is inherent in everyone and that is a strong reason to believe that man did not come about by himself as a result of mere chance or a blind law, but an All-Knowing and Wise Being has created him with a specific purpose. The purpose is that he should nurture his natural instinct, implanted in him as a seed, to open avenues of great progress. This will develop the image of the perfect source of beauty and grace and the only fountainhead of life—i.e. God—in himself and enable him to go on achieving the heights of all kinds of beauty and grace throughout eternity. Think hard: This sense of good and evil inscribed in the *fiṭrah* of every man, and this hidden fountain of light that illuminates the heart of every human being, can never be the result of blind chance or mindless evolution. It clearly proves that the Creator of this natural instinct is a Conscious Being with a decretive will, who has created man for the purpose that he develop this natural instinct to merit higher rewards. I cannot imagine that anyone with an iota of the ability to reflect can call this inherent sense of good and evil, present in every human being, merely a result of chance or natural evolution.

Some say that this universe is like a machine and its

components work automatically in their respective spheres according to their purpose, thus concluding that there is no God. They should think honestly, can this inherent sense that makes everyone inclined to do good be the result of a blind mechanism? Is there, or can there be, a machine that can distinguish between the poor and the rich, the fortunate and the unfortunate, the young and the old, the frail and the strong and the orphan and the non-orphan? Take for instance a flour-grinding machine: will it grind better and faster for a person who is poor or unfortunate or old or frail or orphaned than for a rich or well-off or young and robust man, or a child with living parents? If there is no such machine, and there cannot be one, then does not the inherent sense of good and evil, and man's natural liking for good and for a show of mercy, love, forgiveness, or helping the afflicted, or making a sacrifice under appropriate circumstances, prove that human life is not operating automatically like a machine, but that there is another Being who has inscribed these emotions in his *fiṭrah* with a particular purpose?

Similarly, it is part of human nature for man to view evil with abhorrence; and he feels remorse if he happens to commit evil while he is unmindful or provoked. This also proves that human life is not machine-like; rather, some Higher Being has created it with a particular purpose, and natural guards have been appointed over the citadel of his heart with a special purpose. A wealth of emotions is embedded in man's heart and the knowledge of proper and improper use of each emotion is also sown in his nature and so is the tendency to opt for the proper use and shun its improper use under all circumstances. The law or Shariah is always revealed to nurture these hidden seeds in human *fiṭrah*.

In short, the knowledge of good and evil, which is inherent in human nature, is strong evidence that man did not come into existence by himself and his life is not machine-like; rather, in the background there is an intelligent Being with a determined will who has created him with a purpose.

If at this point someone asks the question, is it not possible that this sense, referred to as the innate sense, might be the result of surrounding circumstances, as well as family and national traditions—that is to say, this liking for good and aversion to evil may not be inherent, but that it was something humans learnt through experiencing what is good and bad and, after a long time, this became established in their minds and appears as if it is inherent—the answer to this is that although this criticism appears worthy of consideration, if we examine it carefully it becomes obvious that there are only two ways of acquiring the knowledge of good and evil: either by long-term experience and the effects of our surroundings, as the questioner thinks, or by bestowal from a Higher Being, as Islam teaches us—one cannot think of a third way. What we have to do now is see which of the two is correct and based on reality. The first thing we notice is that there is a kind of uniformity about this knowledge of good and evil, regardless of the people or the times; i.e. this understanding in its essence appears to be similar in its form and style among every people and during every age. This clearly proves that it could not be the result of experience and impact of our surroundings, but has been bestowed upon human nature by an external power which is supreme and above all. Anything that develops as a result of experience and environmental factors must vary from people to people and from time to time, especially in

the earliest days when different peoples were unaware of one
another and lacked social interaction, because every people's
experience and conditions differ from one another. So this sense
should definitely have developed differently in various peoples.
We observe that national customs and ways, which are certainly
shaped by environmental circumstances, differ in various peoples. Thus, if the realisation of good and evil were based on the
conditions and experience of people, it would have varied from
people to people and from time to time. However, this is not
the case; rather, this sense has always been seen in every age and
among every people to be the same, meaning in the condition of
uniformity. Take, for instance, two peoples with completely different circumstances, one cultured, educated, and civilised and
the other primitive, ignorant, and uncivilised. Despite this degree
of difference, as far as the mere realisation [of good and evil] is
concerned, it will be one and the same, and the differences, if
any, will be in matters relating to its subsequent development;
i.e. it would appear to have developed in one particular form and
direction in one people and in a different form and direction
in the other. However, when they are viewed independently of
later effects, in essence they would appear the same in their form
and style. This proves that the realisation [of good and evil] in
its essence is not brought about by circumstances and experience
but is inherent and no man is deprived of it.

The second proof that the realisation of right and wrong is
inherent rather than acquired is that it appears to be operating
in certain matters wherein it cannot be attributed, by any wise
person, to experience and surroundings. In other words, these
matters are such that their benefit or loss cannot be ascertained

by human experience in any way; any realisation about them can never be attributed to experience and circumstances but will undoubtedly be taken as originating from a Higher Being, who has wisely bestowed it upon every human being. For instance, we see that some form of respect for the dead body has been prevalent throughout the ages among all people. Obviously, by its very nature, this has nothing to do with experience and environment and cannot be attributed to anything except natural instinct. In short, the comprehension of good and evil, relating to matters that have never been experienced and seem to carry no material advantage, is clear evidence that such a sense of awareness is not a learned behaviour but is an inherent trait infused into human nature by a Higher Being.

The third proof that the sense of good and evil is inherent is that in certain instances it manifests itself in a manner that is against national traditions, thereby it cannot be attributed to the latter as the effect can never be at odds with the causative agent. There are many examples found in history where, for instance, over a long period a nation becomes hard-hearted due to certain circumstances and its members become inclined towards ruthlessness and rigidity; national traditions make every member hard-hearted, merciless, and heartless. Nevertheless, a careful study of their nature, psychology, and life history will reveal a feeling of mercy covered by the veil of this heartlessness and this will be seen manifested from time to time, one way or another. Similarly, there are instances when a nation has passed through circumstances which have nurtured the feelings of mercy, forgiveness, and tenderness to an extent that, for every member, national traditions have become synonymous with mercy. However, a careful study will reveal that everyone in that nation would feel that if reformation requires harshness and punishment while forgiveness and mercy is detrimental, then one should resort to harshness as the appropriate punishment rather than forgiveness and mercy. In short, at times this knowledge of good and evil is also found at odds with a nation's condition and indigenous traditions, and this is so because that is the part of *fiṭrah* which may be suppressed by circumstances but can never die. That is why it is observed many a time that the family and national circumstances mould someone's disposition into a kind of a new nature that can be called a 'second nature'. Even then, fundamental nature, when stirred, erupts through the veils of the second nature like a pent up volcano.

To summarise, indeed the circumstances and traditions lead to the development of a kind of nature, but that is a second nature and not the basic nature, or *fiṭrah*. The latter has nothing to do with national circumstances, traditions, or experiences but is part of human constitution. *Fiṭrah,* which has been bestowed with the knowledge of good and evil in an extremely judicious manner, is clear evidence that there is a rational Creator of this *fiṭrah* who has inscribed this element in it with a definite purpose. The Holy Quran says:

$$\text{فَاَلْهَمَهَا فُجُورَهَا وَ تَقْوٰىهَا}^{1}$$

God has invested the *fiṭrah* of every man with the knowledge of

---

1. *Sūrah ash-Shams,* 91:9.

good and evil and has told him through his *fiṭrah* that this is the good way and this is the evil way.

Again it says:

وَهَدَيْنٰهُ النَّجْدَيْنِ ١

We showed man the two paths—good and evil (through his *fiṭrah*). Now, it is up to him to follow the way he likes.

Elsewhere it states clearly:

وَ اِذْ اَخَذَ رَبُّكَ مِنْ بَنِيٓ اٰدَمَ مِنْ ظُهُورِهِمْ ذُرِّيَّتَهُمْ وَ اَشْهَدَهُمْ عَلٰى اَنْفُسِهِمْ اَلَسْتُ بِرَبِّكُمْ ۖ قَالُوْا بَلٰى ۛ شَهِدْنَا ۚ اَنْ تَقُوْلُوْا يَوْمَ الْقِيٰمَةِ اِنَّا كُنَّا عَنْ هٰذَا غٰفِلِيْنَ ٢

And remember the time when your Lord brought forth from the loins of the sons of Ādam their offspring and made them witnesses against their own selves by saying, 'Am I not your Lord?' They replied, 'Indeed, You are our Lord'. This He did lest you say on the Day of Resurrection, 'We were unaware of the existence of our God'.

In short, the knowledge of good and evil exists in the *fiṭrah* of every man; this inherent knowledge substantiates that man did not come into being by himself nor is he the product of a blind law. This is such a clear proof of God's existence that it cannot be denied by any reasonable person.

---

1. *Sūrah al-Balad*, 90:11.

2. *Sūrah al-Aʿrāf*, 7:173.

Evidence of Universal Acceptance

The next argument that I would like to present is that of general acceptance. It is based on the principle that worldwide acceptance of a notion or a belief that has survived throughout the ages is evidence that such a notion or belief, in its essence, is based on truth. The Holy Quran states:

فَاَمَّا الزَّبَدُ فَيَذْهَبُ جُفَآءً ۚ وَ اَمَّا مَا يَنْفَعُ النَّاسَ فَيَمْكُثُ فِي الْاَرْضِ ۚ [1]

That which is really useful and beneficial for the people constantly persists in the world, but a useless and unbeneficial thing never achieves that permanence.

Likewise, we have the scientific principle of 'survival of the fittest'; i.e. in the struggle for survival, only what is useful and worthy of survival prospers and the rest perishes. Our observation also suggests that only beneficial things attain real longevity and a harmful, useless, or non-beneficial thing cannot flourish worldwide indefinitely. I do not mean to say that a false or non-beneficial thing cannot be established in the world; rather, my point is that the existence of such a thing cannot be permanent and worldwide and that its existence is temporary and limited.

When viewed according to this principle, belief in God turns out to be a doctrine that cannot be denied by any sensible person. All the nations in the world, great or small, civilised or uncivilised, educated or uneducated, all of them wherever they are, despite their innumerable differences, agree that this universe did not just

---

1. *Sūrah ar-Raʿd*, 13:18.

happen; rather, it has a Creator and a Master. The notion that this universe is created and owned by a Higher Being is not limited to present-day nations only, but has been seen among all nations without exception throughout recorded history. Granted, there is a great deal of disagreement over the attributes of that Higher Being, and different nations present God in different forms and shapes; some believe in one God with no other deity above or below Him, while others have many deities and insist on devotion to all of them. In short, there is a great deal of disagreement about the Being of God and His attributes among different nations. But despite this disagreement, the focal point of religions of all nations appears to be this: the universe did not come into being by itself; rather, it is the miracle of Omnipotence of a Higher Being. The Jews and the Christians, the Hindus and the Muslims, the Sikhs and the Parsīs, the Jains and the Buddhists, the Native Americans of North America, the Hottentots and the Zulus of South Africa, indigenous people of West Africa and Aborigines of Australia, the Eskimos of the Arctic, the Maoris of New Zealand, the Gonds and the Santhals of India, and the Taoists of China—when we look upon epochs, we see the people of the present age or the middle ages or the pre-historic ages or the primitive tribes—in short, take whatever nation and whichever period of time and the belief that this universe is governed by some Higher Being comes to light in one form or another. Therefore, this consensus on the existence of God among all nations throughout the ages, the great and numerous disagreements notwithstanding and no matter what His attributes are and whether He is one or more than one, constitutes evidence of the existence of God which no intelligent person can deny. I am not saying that these nations

claim to have seen or recognised God and perceived His attributes
as eyewitnesses. All I say is that all nations of the world, despite
innumerable religious differences, have proclaimed belief in God,
in one form or another, throughout the ages, and this claim alone,
because of its universal acceptance, constitutes an argument supporting the existence of God.

Consider carefully that such universal acceptance of a belief—
that all nations proclaim it as a focal point of their faiths, and the
failure to find a single instance in recorded history of a nation as
a whole rejecting this belief—indeed constitutes an undeniable
argument for the truth of said belief. Wrong beliefs do take root
in the world; sometimes they disseminate widely over a certain
period but never has it been observed that such a wrong belief
has spread all over the world so as to engulf all nations without
exception, and never beyond a limited period in such a way as to
have acquired universal acceptance since the beginning of days. If
that happened, peace would vanish from this world and it would
become difficult to distinguish truth from falsehood. Hence, the
widespread and overwhelming acceptance of this belief—i.e. that
there is a Higher Being ruling over this universe who is beyond
the limitations of time and space—and the wonderful longevity
of this belief, unparalleled in the history of the world, attests that
the belief in a Higher Being cannot be false.

Indeed, during all of the ages there have been, there are people who did not believe in any God at all. However, they never
attained the status of a nation for any length of time and atheism
has never been proclaimed as state religion anywhere; neither has
an atheistic movement ever been launched as an independent and
well-grounded movement. It has never attained any significance

beyond temporarily taking over the hearts and minds of a few men. In the history of nations, the doctrine of atheism can be compared to a small group of insurgents who revolt from time to time against an organised and established government, but cannot hold out for long; nor do they manage to achieve any lasting and strong sovereignty over any significant territory. Can the authority of any established government be challenged on account of such rebels? No, never!

Is Belief in God Based on Superstition?

If at this point someone harbours a doubt that some Western historians claim to have identified some ancient nations who were altogether unaware of the belief in God, then the answer to this is as follows: Granted, some historians have noted this, and, in particular, they have asserted that peoples living in the earliest age were unaware of the belief in God altogether; however, a careful study reveals that such authors have been mistaken and have not fully done their research. Specifically, they have erred in attributing the idolatrous beliefs of certain ancient nations merely to fear, ignorance, and superstition, and concluded from this erroneously that they never believed in one God. That is absolutely incorrect; the fact is that idolatry, though resulting from ignorance, is an offshoot of the belief in God, not its root. That is to say, idolatrous beliefs always result from the corrupted forms of belief in God and never develop in the complete absence of belief in God. There are instances in world history that a nation appears to believe in God initially and, later, idolatrous notions creep in slowly and sometimes take over completely, relegating and annihilating belief in God. In the presence of such examples, justice demands that we assume concerning the primitive nations who appear to be steeped in idolatrous beliefs—while we do not have their historical records—that they subscribed to belief in God initially, which later degenerated into idolatrous beliefs. In fact, the examples presented by some to negate our view relate to the nations whose earliest historical records have not been preserved. In this situation, it would be unfair to ignore other clear-cut instances and conclude that those nations held idolatrous views from the very beginning and that their idolatrous beliefs were based merely on ignorance, fear, and superstition, and that belief in one God never took root among them; such a conclusion would be unacceptable to any unbiased, reasonable person.

Moreover, if we ponder, we see that idolatrous beliefs can never arise out of ignorance, fear, and superstition alone; a belief in God must pre-exist. It is natural for one to be awestruck when confronted with something that is more powerful, formidable, magnificent, or beneficial than him; he begins to consider it as an immense thing and is subdued by it and fears it. However, if he is unacquainted with the concept of worship, it is absolutely impossible for him to take something as a deity out of awe or fear only, and regard it as his creator and master; for the thought of worship to occur, the concept of worship must pre-exist in his mind. Human imagination can never create a concept; it can certainly imitate. That is, if someone has seen or heard or experienced something, his perception can create its image in his mind, which he can develop and expand further. However, if he has never seen or heard it, nor witnessed the like of it, his perception cannot create its image in his mind. Therefore, as the concept of the worshipper and the worshipped exists in the belief structure of every nation, inevitably we have to accept that every nation in essence subscribes to belief in God.

Someone may say that at the start of this treatise it was stated emphatically that these days most of the people do not believe in God and every nation is falling prey to atheism, whereas now we are being told that all nations of the world believe in God and that atheism never enjoyed this general acceptance, and that this is an obvious contradiction. But this is not the case. When it was said that all nations are falling prey to atheism, it was with a view to actual belief, and here we are discussing the doctrine, not actual belief. Thus, the two statements are not contradictory, as both are correct in their respective contexts. It is true that most of the people these days do not believe in God inasmuch as their belief is not a living reality and it does not affect their lives. It is also true that all nations in the world have been subscribing to belief in God in one way or the other as part of their belief systems. For, however weak and lifeless, rather idolatrous, their belief might have been, they have always maintained that there is a God over this universe who governs our lives. Obviously we are talking about the doctrine not profound insight. So both statements are correct in their appropriate contexts and there is no contradiction. To summarise, the magnificent and worldwide acceptance enjoyed by the doctrine of belief in God throughout the ages is evidence that it is based on truth and that the opposing doctrine of atheism is incorrect and false.

Three Grades of Certainty

The next argument I would like to present in favour of God, albeit logical and relating to the 'ought-to-be' stage of certainty concerning God, provides a sure and definite sign to God for the discerning. One must not assume that logical arguments are just hypothetical and cannot lead to any degree of certainty concerning God. Anyone who has this idea has completely misunderstood. The 'ought-to-be' stage concerning God is a stage of certainty, just as the 'is' stage is a stage of certainty. The difference is that the 'ought-to-be' stage does not provide the utmost certainty provided by the 'is' stage, and it is not as assuring and as comforting; nevertheless, no wise person should doubt that it is a stage of certainty.

There are various stages of certainty. One stage of certainty is that which is achieved by reasoning, when we infer the existence of something by observing some of its effects. For instance, when we observe smoke far off in a forest, we infer that there is a fire giving off smoke, as there cannot be smoke without fire, and that gives us the certainty of reason. In Quranic terminology this is called *'ilmul-yaqīn;* i.e. the certainty through inference in the absence of any direct observation. Clearly, the 'ought to be' stage belongs to this category, as we infer the existence of God from signs, not from direct observation. When we see fire with our eyes, or experience its heat, the 'ought to be' stage of certainty changes to 'is' stage of definitive certainty. In other words, in the 'ought to be' stage we believe in God on the basis of reasoning and in the 'is' stage we no longer depend on reasoning; rather, we graduate to a kind of physical observation.

It would not be out of place to mention the other two stages of certainty described by the Holy Quran. The first, as mentioned above, is that of *'ilmul-yaqīn,* in which certainty about something is acquired by logical inference from its signs. The second stage is that of *'aynul-yaqīn* [the certainty of sight], which marks the beginning of observation and no longer requires reasoning. For instance, when we walk in the direction of the smoke and begin to see the fire with our eyes, then we do not have *'ilmul-yaqīn* only, but acquire *'aynul-yaqīn;* i.e. we believe on the authority of direct observation and inference plays no part in it.

There is another stage above this, called *ḥaqqul-yaqīn* [the certainty of experience] in Quranic terminology. This stage is reached when man gets so close to the fire that he experiences its heat and not only sees the fire but also benefits from its heat and can distinguish the right path from the wrong one in its light. This is the ultimate stage of certainty beyond which there is no other stage. Although there are several sub-stages within this ultimate stage and everyone attains their place according to their capacity and effort. We need not go into the details here. In short, there are several stages of certainty, and the stage of 'ought to be', called *'ilmul-yaqīn,* the one we are discussing here, is an elementary stage.

The Inevitable Victory of Prophets

Throughout the recorded history of the world, we observe that whenever those who believe in God have been defied by those who deny God (in doctrine or practically), the former have always triumphed. This demonstrates that some hidden power helps the believers. I do not mean to say that a believer triumphs against a disbeliever in every contest under all circumstances, as ordinarily, victory or defeat follows the laws of nature, and there is no reason why a disbeliever who follows the path of success should not triumph against a believer who does not. Ordinarily, success belongs to one who treads along the path of success. I do not have in mind ordinary worldly differences and contests, but I mean that whenever someone proclaims that he has been commissioned by God to establish faith in the world, he certainly succeeds in his mission and no worldly power can block his path to success. The Holy Quran says:

$$\text{كَتَبَ اللهُ لَأَغْلِبَنَّ أَنَا وَ رُسُلِيْ} ^{1}$$

That is, Allah has decreed that He and His Messengers will always prevail.

Accordingly, we observe that a Messenger takes the field all alone. In material terms, he is absolutely helpless, whereas his adversaries, on account of their numbers and provisions, appear as if they will crush him in no time. But gradually his powerful message is accepted by the people and ultimately he triumphs and his opponents are thoroughly humiliated. The world has witnessed this scenario not once, not twice, not tens of times, not hundreds of times, but thousands of times. There is not a single example recorded in the history of the world where an atheist triumphed

---

1. *Sūrah al-Mujādalah,* 58:22.

in such a dispute (by atheist I mean one who either denies God or believes in Him ritually but not in reality).

My dear ones! A battle [of ideas] takes place in different parts of the world, in different nations, at different times, under different circumstances, not tens of times, not hundreds of times, but thousands of times. On each occasion, a helpless and ill-equipped man of God takes a stand in the name of God against a large, well-equipped army of disbelievers. The battle starts and the man of God emerges triumphant and the army of atheism is taken prisoner and has to join his disciples. Is this all by chance? Give just one example wherein the host of disbelievers emerged victorious and the man of God was humiliated in such a battle. Does this scenario not provide convincing evidence that those who stand in the name of God are supported by the hand of an Omnipotent Being against whom material means amount to nothing at all?

See the exploits of Krishan [Krishna] and Ram Chandra Ji in India. What did these great men stand for and how did the ungrateful people of India treat them? What was the result? Do the Aryas not bow down to these holy personages in submission today?

Look at the life history of the Patriarch Prophet Ibrāhīm[as] [Abraham], the Friend of Allah. This man of God stood up all alone proclaiming God in the dark valleys of Syria. The stalwarts of atheism responded by casting him into a burning fire. However, that apparently helpless man felt no fear and continued to sing the praises of God as if he were lying on a bed of roses. Why? Because Ibrāhīm[as] could hear the Divine voice reverberating in his ears: 'O Ibrāhīm! Look at the sky; can you count those stars?' Ibrāhīm[as] replied: 'My Lord, who can count your hosts?' God said: 'O Ibrāhīm! You have made a covenant of love and loyalty with Us; We do now swear in Our own Name that your progeny will become, and shine as, stars of the sky of [divine] guidance and no one will be able to count them'. Look around! Today, the followers of Ibrāhīm[as] outnumber those of any other Prophet, but where are those who threw him in the fire?

Take Mūsā[as] [Moses] next. A child was born to a poor family. His household, for fear of Pharaoh, placed him in a basket and cast him into the river. He was picked up by Pharaoh's people and, out of mercy or some other reason, he was brought up in Pharaoh's house by his command. When he grew up, he had to flee the country, fearing punishment for violating the law of the land on one occasion. Wandering around in the wilderness, he ended up serving a pious man for ten years, after which he married. Then, after being Divinely enlightened, he returned to Pharaoh's court and told him face-to-face, 'I am a Messenger of the God who created you and me and all others; send the Israelites with me or your end will not be good'. Pharaoh, who was intoxicated with power, frowned and said, 'O Mūsā! You dare speak to me in this manner, having grown up on the leftovers of my household; come to your senses and then speak!' Mūsā[as] realised that the intoxicated goliath would not come to his senses. He planned to escape tactfully with the Israelites under the cover of secrecy, whatever the consequences. Pharaoh learnt about this and was outraged. He pursued the escapees in the wilderness, accompanied by his large armies, and quickly caught up with them. The Israelites, rendered cowardly after years of enslavement, got frightened seeing Pharaoh's armies behind them and the dreadful sea in front. 'What will happen next?', they asked. Mūsā[as] was unmoved like a rock; he looked at those frightened faces and said:

$$\text{إِنَّ مَعِيَ رَبِّي سَيَهْدِينِ}^{1}$$

That is: Nay, there is nothing to worry about, my Lord is with me. He will find some way out for us.

Glory be to Allah! It is the same Mūsā[as], who had fled from Egypt for fear of the authorities a few years earlier, now facing the Pharaoh's army and remains absolutely unruffled. What happened next? The sea parted to make way for Mūsā[as] while Pharaoh and his army, with all its armament, were engulfed by the dreadful sea waves. And it did not end there; like Ibrāhīm[as], the followers of Mūsā[as] are beyond count, while no one cares for Pharaoh, though his mummified remains serve as a constant warning to the people.

Let us now look at Masīḥ[as] [the Messiah] of Nazareth. He was born to a poor unmarried Israelite woman; this lead to much gossip among the evil-minded Jews—she was unmarried, whence did the boy come? They forgot that the birth was in fulfilment of an old prophecy.[2] They also forgot that this boy at least had a mother, whereas according to them, Adam had neither a mother nor a father. However, this fatherless boy grew up and with the support of the Holy Spirit proclaimed what Krishna[as] had asserted in India, Ibrāhīm[as] in Syria, and Mūsā[as] in Egypt. The Jews who were already weary about him became furious and ultimately he was put on the cross as a result of their intrigues. The Jews were

---

1. *Sūrah ash-Shuʿarāʾ,* 26:63.
2. Isaiah 7:14.

happy to have carried the day. But Masīḥ[as] had the backing of One
who came to his assistance, saved him from a humiliating death,
and comforted him, saying: 'It was expedient to give temporary
dominance to the Jews but I am your faithful Lord and your disciples will hold sway over the Jews till the end of the days; the world
will witness that it is you who really prevailed and not the Jews'.
What does the world see today? Have not the disciples of Masīḥ[as]
overwhelmed the whole world? In what state are the Jews? Those
same Jews who once crowned Masīḥ[as] [the Messiah] with thorns
and ridiculed him, saying, look at him, he is our 'king'; today, the
servants of Masīḥ[as], out of mercy, want to crown the Jews with the
kingdom of the Holy Land, but no one is allowing it;[1] the whole
nation of Israelites has been on the cross, as it were, for nineteen
centuries, for having put Masīḥ[as] on the cross for a few hours.
Glory be to Allah! What an exemplary retribution!

Then, look at the Chief of them all: Muhammad Muṣṭafā
[the Chosen One], peace and blessings of Allah be on him (and
may my life be sacrificed for him). A youth from a respecta-
ble but poor Quraish family is married to a virtuous woman.
Husband and wife live together for only a short period when she
loses her husband. She is pregnant and distressed at her dreadful
loss. The child is born, prompting mixed emotions of intense
pain of missing her husband and the feeling of joy of holding a
baby who will keep her husband's name alive. In keeping with
Quraish traditions she wants to hand him over to a Bedouin wet
nurse, but who will accept an orphan? After a prolonged search,

---

1. This treatise was written during the Zionist movement but prior to the
   creation of the State of Israel. [Publisher]

at last, they find a wet nurse willing to take the child with her, and thus does the Chief of all the Prophets spend the early days of his life in a desert hut. When he grows a bit older, he returns to his mother. But not long afterwards, she reunites in the Hereafter with her deceased husband, and this boy is left without a mother or a father. He is brought up by some of his relatives till he becomes a young man, and, like rest of the Quraish, he takes up trading as his career, and thus the years pass by. He is illiterate and unlettered, but respected for his high morals—and people address him with the title of *Amīn* [the Trustworthy]. As he approaches forty, he becomes inclined to solitude and his virtuous nature despises the customs and beliefs of the Quraish. He searches for a high moral code and truly satisfying faith. He chooses a desolate cave in a desolate mountain near Makkah for his solitude. He spends his days and nights there, in remembrance of an unknown being who would provide bliss to his anxious heart. He has no one to confide in except his aging wife, who lives in Makkah, and becomes concerned about the state of her worried husband. Thus it proceeds till one day, the brilliant rays of that Unknown Being, for whom he had been searching, reaches out to his pure heart and the expansive scenario of the spiritual world starts unfolding before him.

Not long afterwards, he emerges from this veil of secrecy and declares his God-given station to the Quraish and calls them to God, who is the Creator and Master of this universe, besides whom there is no God. They laugh at this and do not take him seriously. However, he perseveres and some sensible, faithful people gather around him, believe in him, and help him in his cause. The people soon realise that they cannot just laugh

this call off, and, if not controlled, it will divide their nation
and cause dissension. This starts a magnificent war, unparalleled in world history, that rocks and ravages the Arab world for
twenty years, and kindles a fire from one end of the country to
the other that is not extinguished until the whole country gath-
ers under the banner of the One God. At first, the Quraish of
Makkah tried to coerce the handful of Muslims back to their
old faith, and subjected them to tyrannies, the accounts of which
make one's hair stand on end. Bilal[ra] was an Abyssinian slave,
of righteous nature, who accepted Islam immediately. His master, Umayyah bin Khalf, tortured him most brutally. This evil
one laid him stripped naked on the sand under the hot midday
sun, when the earth was scorching hot, placed large stones on
his chest, mounted them, and said: part with Muhammad[saw],
stop worshipping [one] God and prostrate to the idols, or else I
will torture you like this until death. Bilal[ra] was not well-versed
in Arabic; he would look to the heavens and say: *Aḥad! Aḥad!*
This meant: God is One; God is One; I cannot leave Him. Then
the tyrant would tie him up with a rope and hand him over to
street hooligans, who would drag him along the stony streets of
Makkah, whereby his unclothed body was wounded and bled
profusely. Umayyah would ask him again: what do you say now?
Bilal[ra] would utter the same words again: *Aḥad! Aḥad!* That
is: God is One; God is One. The street boys, with a nod from
Umayyah, would drag him over the scorching stones again.

Another Muslim, Khubāb[ra] by name, not a slave, worked as
a blacksmith in Makkah. The outraged wicked youth of Quraish
would lay him on the burning coals of his furnace; one person
would mount on his chest to prevent him turning to his side till

the coals burned out under his back. However, this faithful servant did not give up God. Samiyyah[ra] was a poor Muslim woman. Abu Jahl intimidated her, [saying] give up Islam or else I will torture you to death, but she declined and held fast to Islam. Ultimately, the vicious man thrust a spear into her private parts and martyred her in the scorching fields of Makkah. These are but a few early narratives of the religious war waged by the Quraish of Makkah against the poor and helpless Muslims.

The master and leader of the Muslims (may my life be sacrificed for him) was himself stoned by the wicked people of Taif and extensively wounded from head to toe, till his shoes were filled with his own blood. He was socially boycotted in Makkah in an effort to kill him. When these atrocities reached their climax and the Quraish decided to assassinate Muhammad[saw] at all costs, to bring an end to it all, the Holy Prophet[saw], accompanied by some of his followers, migrated from Makkah to Madinah to cool off the Quraish, so that they may let the Muslims live in peace and they may continue their peaceful preaching unhindered. But this infuriated the Quraish even more, and their leaders went around the country stirring up the Arab tribes against the Muslims, leaving them, as it were, trapped in a bushfire without an escape route. The following historical narrative depicts the condition of the Muslims at the time:

When Muhammad[saw] and his followers arrived and were given asylum in Madinah, the whole of Arabia rose up united against them. Those days the Muslims slept with their weapons at the ready and carried their weapons during daytime for fear of an enemy attack at any time. Greatly

distressed, they used to say: When shall we see the days
wherein we shall live in peace and tranquillity and fear no
one other than God. (*Lubābun-naqūl fi asbābun-nuzūl*)

At that time, the Muslims were no more than a handful—mostly
poor, weak, and ill-equipped. They were confronted by the well-
equipped, united forces of the whole country, surging against
them like a great deluge to wipe them off the face of the earth.

The sacrifices that the Holy Prophet, peace and blessings
of Allah be on him, and his[saw] Companions had to make and
the hardships they had to endure during this unique struggle
are recorded in every authentic history book and need not be
repeated here. There is one incident, however, that I cannot leave
out. The Holy Prophet, peace and blessings of Allah be on him,
was passing through a valley in Hejaz, accompanied by a large
party, when an enemy tribe suddenly unleashed a volley of arrows.
The Muslim allies retreated in the face of this unexpected attack,
creating panic in the Muslim army; the camels, horses, mules,
and donkeys along with their riders turned back and fled hel-
ter-skelter. The enemy noticed this, roared forward and started
raining arrows on the fleeing Muslims. The Holy Prophet, peace
and blessings of Allah be on him, looked around and found the
battlefield deserted—not the new converts of Makkah, nor the
faithful *Ansār* [Helpers] of Madinah, nor the old *Muhājirīn*
[Emigrants] were to be seen. There was only the enemy surging
forward like a great deluge and arrows rained incessantly; but he
stood his ground like a mountain and very calmly told his frightened companion who was standing nearby to hold the rein of his

horse lest it turn back in the face of arrows and spurred his horse forward towards the enemy shouting:

انا النبيّ لا كذب   انا ابن عبد المطلب

Meaning, I am the Prophet of God, not a liar.[1]

As if by magic, all the Muslims who heard this voice scrambled and fought their way back and gathered around their master and shattered the advancing columns of the enemy. In short, this war surely took place; nine years had not gone by since the recluse of the Cave of Hira took refuge in Madinah that the vast land of Arabia—nine hundred thousand square miles of it—was reverberating with the slogans of *takbīr* [i.e. God's greatness] from one end to the other.

One might say this was all due to the sword; I say, show me how you would achieve such a result with the sword! One man— all alone, poor, and powerless, weak and impoverished, stands up and, within a few years, transforms the whole country—a country laced with arms from head to toe against him. Is that the work of a sword or the miracle of a protective God?

O naive ones! Who raised the sword? Is there any among you who can prove that Muslims were the first to use the sword? Again, is there any among you who can prove that, when Muslims did use the sword to defend themselves and establish peace, they converted a single person to Islam with the sword? O unfortunate

---

1. The second Arabic statement, not translated by the author, reads, 'I am the son of Abdul Muttalib', who was the Prophet's[saw] paternal grandfather. [Publisher]

sons of darkness! How can I convince you that it was the Arabs who unsheathed the sword against the Muslims and that they did not sheathe it until they realised that Muhammad^{saw} had the backing of a powerful Being, against whom these material means do not matter as much as the wing of a gnat. Indeed, they accepted Islam out of fear—not that of the sword, but of God. Indeed, they broke their idols with their own hands, not because they were afraid of Muslim power but because they observed the idols humiliated and helpless. History tells us that, after the fall of Makkah, when the idols were broken, some of the chiefs of Makkah looked at the idols contemptuously and said: If these idols had any power, the stiff-necked Arabs would not bow down to Muhammad^{saw} today.[1] This is what was said by those in the thick of it and you—more than thirteen centuries later, living thousands of miles away from Arabia, and absolutely ignorant of Islamic history—claim that the Arabs accepted Islam for fear of the sword of Muhammad (peace and blessings of Allah be on him)! Woe be to prejudice! Is there no limit to unfairness?

In short this phenomenal success of the Holy Prophet, peace and blessings of Allah be on him, is clear proof of the fact that there was a powerful Being working in support of him, and He is the very Being whom we call God. Now, thirteen-and-a-half centuries after his death, four hundred million people take pride in his servitude and the number is ever increasing.[2] That day is not far off when, by the grace of God, this incomparable king of the

---

1. *Tārīkhul-Khamīs.*

2. This number has since quadrupled to 1.6 billion Muslims throughout the world per the Pew Research Center. [Publisher]

spiritual realm will rule the hearts of the whole world with his God-given splendour, and the heads of the Arabs and the non-Arabs will bow down in servitude of love before this man, who was a veritable *zill-ullāh* [reflection of Allah]. وياايُها اللهم صلّ عليه وآله وسلّم. ـالذين آمنوا صلُّوا عليه وسلّموا تسليما [O Allah, bless Muhammad and his people and bestow peace on him. O ye who believe! Invoke blessings on him and salute him with the salutation of peace].

After the Holy Prophet, peace and blessings of Allah be on him (may my life be sacrificed for him), his servant, perfect *zill* [shadow], and beautiful *burūz* [reflection], the person of Ḥaḍrat Mirza Ghulam Ahmad of Qadian, peace be upon him, with sublime qualities, is also a holy link in this chain [of Prophets]. A child is born in a backward village in India which had poor facilities of communication—train or postal services. He grew under the loving care of his parents but, being inclined to solitude, distanced himself even from the limited social circle of the village. The father, out of his paternal kindness, tries to arrange a good job for him and sends a message to him: a certain high official is a good friend of mine and he is in charge these days; I could speak to him and arrange a reasonable job for you. He gets the reply: Do not worry about me; I have found employment at the place I am meant to be. That is to say: I am in service to God; I do not need any worldly employment. With this begins the tale of the sacred mission that has created upheaval in the religious world today.

Ḥaḍrat Mirza Ghulam Ahmad[as] claimed to be a *Mujaddid* [Reformer] in 1884. There was nothing in the claim that would startle the Muslims as there had been many *mujaddids* in the Islamic world. Therefore, the claim was met with silent acceptance, or at least was not rejected. He continued to serve Islam in accordance with His God-given mandate and the sensible among the Muslims looked upon his services with gratitude. They realised that he was the only one among the Muslims who had the ability to stand up to the enemies successfully and respectably. However, it stirred up a dangerous fervour of animosity and opposition among anti-Islamic factions—i.e. the Hindus and the Christians—and they resolved to hurt him and bring him down by every possible means. Not long afterwards, Ḥaḍrat Mirza Ghulam Ahmad[as], on Divine command, proclaimed that he was the fulfilment of prophecies concerning the Latter-Day Messiah and Imam Mahdi, and that Masīḥ[as] [the Messiah] of Nazareth, whose second advent was being awaited, had died. He further claimed that he was the Promised Reformer of the Latter Days, as mentioned in the prophecies of different religions. His task was to confront and overcome falsehood and bring about the supremacy of truth. He claimed to be the Promised One foretold by all religions, through whom the final and worldwide victory of Islam is decreed.

This claim caused a great commotion and all faiths became united in an unprecedented manner in opposition to him. The other Muslims, the Christians, the Hindus, the Aryas, the Jains, the Sikhs, the Brahmūs, the Dev Samājīsts, etc. took to the field with all their might against an ill-equipped person, all on his own. Most of the Muslim ulama declared him to be an infidel, heretic, himself misled and misguiding others; and, in fact, they called him *Dajjāl* [the antichrist]. An edict was issued and circulated throughout the Islamic world to the effect that this man was an infidel and outside the pale of Islam—in fact, the worst enemy of Islam. Anyone dealing with him in anyway would also become labelled as being out of the pale of Islam. And it was widely publicized that hurting him in any way was not only justified but in fact a good deed worthy of great merit; some even went as far as declaring that the Islamic Shariah prescribed the penalty of death for him and the one who brings about his death would merit Divine reward. In addition to this vocal opposition, which was not merely vocal as it kindled a veritable and dangerous firestorm of opposition in the country, practically all legal and illegal means were used in an effort to suppress and humiliate him. All of the Muslims, Christians, Hindus, and others attacked him with full force.

The early history of Ahmadiyyat is a tragic story that makes your hair stand on end. On one side was a single person, all alone, apparently without any backing, lacking means, without funds, and without any claim to fame; and on the other hand, it seemed as if there were entire armies of the world, laced with all possible means, surging upon him from all sides like a deluge, yet the man was neither scared nor alarmed but stood his ground like a firm rock. He had no sword to wield, no apparent money to distribute, no worldly knowledge to impress the people with, and no power to intimidate them with—all he had was a spiritual flag with the following words, inscribed with an ink not of this earth:

دُنیا میں ایک نذیر آیا پر دُنیا نے اُس کو قبول نہ کیا لیکن خُدا اُسے قبول کرے گا اور
بڑے زور آور حملوں سے اُس کی سچائی ظاہر کردے گا۔

A Warner came unto the world, but the world accepted him not; yet God shall accept him and demonstrate his truthfulness with mighty assaults. (*Barāhīn-e-Aḥmadiyya*, Part IV, Urdu ed. Ruhānī Khazā'in, p. 655)

As the enemy offensive intensified to dangerous levels, he raised this heavenly flag higher and higher in his hands. There seemed to be some magic in these words: on seeing them, the soldiers of the opposing army began deserting their ranks and instead began to gather around this flag. The opponents harassed these people in every way—punished them socially, snatched their wealth and belongings, split up their families, assaulted them, and even killed some of them. They prevented them from burying their dead in their [Muslim] cemeteries. But such was the effect upon these people that they were readily drawn towards this flag. They were eager to relinquish their apparent freedom in exchange for servitude to this helpless, unknown villager.

Glory be to God! What a spectacle! The opponents said that this was a gnat bothering them with its buzz. If it did not stop buzzing, they would crush it between their fingers. But today the followers of that 'buzzing' are attacking every citadel in the world, and even the enemies admit that if there is any force worth mentioning in the religious world today, this alone is it. Can this be the work of a human being? No, never. Man's work is dependent upon resources and circumstances. In this case, all of the resources were with the enemy, and the Promised Messiah[as] had nothing with him. But despite the enemy's utmost efforts, the Promised Messiah's strong message attracts the hearts of the people. At the time of his passing in 1908, he had 400,000 faithful devotees under his banner. Now, seventeen years after his passing,[1] his followers have spread

---

1. Though this book was originally published in 1927, as the author notes, it was largely written in 1925, which corresponds to the given reference. [Publisher]

to all countries of the world to preach Islam, and are baffling the world with their unprecedented sacrifices in the cause of God. This is not fiction, but fact. Even the enemy cannot hide under the veil of enmity and prejudice. An unknown villager, without resources, stood up and declared that he had been ordained by God to establish His Majesty. The world rejected him and people of all faiths and nations opposed him with all their might and, intoxicated with their power, believed that in no time they would wipe him off the face of the earth. There were enemies all around—bloodthirsty enemies who had put their differences aside to unite, each one eager to be the first to strike. On the other hand, the one whom they regarded a 'buzzing gnat' or a water bubble was like a drawn sword in the hands of a protective God, killing whomsoever it fell upon and whosoever fell upon it was annihilated. Many strong men challenged the champion of God, but, like kernels of corn crackling in the oven, they were destroyed in no time.

Why, after all, did this happen? Look at the early condition of the Ahmadiyya Community, look at the opposition it faced, study its present condition, and then be fair: was this extraordinary success possible without the support of some Unseen Power? A lone, helpless, and totally ill-equipped figure stands up in the Name of God and, despite intense opposition from the whole world, establishes his authority all over the world within a short period of thirty to forty years, as if he alone rules the religious world. There are Ahmadiyya missions in India, Ceylon [now Sri Lanka], Syria, Palestine, Lebanon, Iran, England, Germany, Holland, Switzerland, Italy, Spain, Trinidad, North America, South America, East Africa, West Africa, Mauritius, Malaya

[Malay Peninsula], Java, Sumatra, and Borneo.[1] These are not missions that are breaking down and tamed by the attacks of the enemies, but each is a force to be reckoned with, the mettle of which has been recognized by the world at large. O ye, looking crookedly at the Ahmadiyya Community and shedding tears of blood with outrage at this astonishing success and bemoaning the progress of Islam, listen:

کیا ہے ہوتا دیکھیۓ آگے آگے   کیا ہے روتا ہے عشق ابتداۓ

Why cry, sir, it is but the beginning of love;
Wait and see what is yet to come!

In short, the success that the Promised Messiah, peace be upon him, and his community is having in the face of adverse circumstances, and the rapidity and astonishing manner in which it is taking place, is manifest evidence of the fact that an Unseen Force that dominates and rules all worldly powers is working in his support, and it is He whom we call God.

To summarise, throughout the recorded history of the world, whenever a righteous person ordained by God stood up in His Name, regardless of what kind of circumstances he encountered, he ultimately prevailed and achieved his purpose; and his enemies, despite their enormous power and materials, were always humiliated. This phenomenon, as I said before, has been observed not once or twice, not tens of times, but thousands of times, and

---

1. The number of Ahmadiyya Muslim missions has increased since and, at present, Ahmadi missionaries are serving Islam in most countries of the world. [Publisher]

never the other way round, not even once. Therefore, this predominance is definite and positive proof that those who stand in the Name of God benefit from the support of a great Unseen Force against which all worldly powers and means pale into insignificance; that force we call God. The whole of humanity needs to submit to Him. May the people understand! How beautifully the Promised Messiah[as] has put it:

قدرت سے اپنی ذات کا دیتا ہے حق ثبوت   اُس بے نشاں کی چہرہ نمائی یہی تو ہے

God provides evidence of His existence with His omnipotence;
For the invisible One that, indeed, is the only way of showing His countenance.

جس بات کو کہے کہ کروں گا میں یہ ضرور   ٹلتی نہیں وہ بات خُدائی یہی تو ہے

When He says that He will certainly do something,
That becomes inevitable; that indeed is Godhood.

Testimony of the Righteous

The last logical argument that I would like to present as evidence for the existence of God relates to the testimony of the righteous. It is based on the principle that many people, whose truthfulness is established and whose sanity is unquestionable, testify that we do have a God whom we have seen and recognised, in the exact same way as we see and recognise other invisible things. Everyone with some sense and experience can understand that testimony is an important means of acquiring knowledge. If we review the vast field of our knowledge, we will realise that a large proportion of our knowledge was not acquired directly but by the narratives of reliable people, authentic books, or newspapers; we have never had the opportunity to personally witness or experience many things. In spite of all that, we have almost the same degree of certainty about these things as we do about information gained by our own observation and experience. There is no reason why it should not be like that. After all, we trust and regard our own observation and experience as reliable, therefore, why should we not accept the observation and experience of a person who has a heart and a mind like us and whose truthfulness is also beyond doubt. We believe in the world news given in newspapers; we accept modern scientific research about the properties of particles, though only very few of us have personally experienced these first-hand. All of the decisions in civil and criminal courts around the world are based on verbal or written testimonies and no one objects to this. Knowledge of history is largely based on verbal or written testimony, and this is accepted by all. Take the knowledge of geography. Everyone in India believes that there is a city called London, which is the capital of England, although less than one percent of the population of India has ever seen London. They believe in it on the basis of other people's testimony. Moreover, practically, in our day-to-day life, we believe in many things only on the testimony of others, though we have no personal knowledge about them.

In short, no sane person can deny that testimony is a major means of acquiring knowledge. Such a denial would render many sciences invalid and useless for most of the world. Rejecting the principle of testimony would mean that people should only believe in matters observed and experienced personally by themselves, and deny the rest. In fact, by rejecting this principle, we cannot remain convinced of any science, because if the observation and experience of Tom, Dick, and Harry—despite being truthful and sane and in the absence of any motive for them to lie—is not acceptable, then there is no reason that our own observation and experience should be acceptable to us. If they can err in their observation, so can we. Thus, it is established that rejection of the principle of testimony can lead to nothing but opening the door for superstition.

One might say that, at times, testimony may be false or incorrect; and, sometimes, although the witness is not a liar, but because he is deemed to lack adequate intelligence and understanding, he cannot be accepted as a reliable witness. This notion is correct and we accept it; however, we cannot reject the role of testimony in the acquisition of knowledge solely because of this possibility. The overall usefulness of medication cannot be refuted if a patient experiences ill effects by using a medicine that is of poor quality or expired. Similarly, we cannot reject the value of testimony because, at times, it may be false or the witness unreliable. We need to conclude that just as it is essential to avoid substandard medicine, we should be cautious in accepting the testimony of liars or unreliable people, as mentioned in the Holy Quran:

$$\text{اِنْ جَآءَكُمْ فَاسِقٌ بِنَبَاٍ فَتَبَيَّنُوْٓا}^{[1]}$$

That is, if a liar brings you any news, do not accept it without investigation, but accept it only if verified by investigation.

---

1. *Sūrah al-Ḥujurāt*, 49:7.

In short, testimony is an important means of acquiring knowledge and it cannot be ignored simply because of the possibility that some testimonies might be incorrect. If something can be rejected because of such a possibility, then nothing in the world would be acceptable. This is because no matter how certain we are about something, there is always the possibility of such kinds of doubts and mistakes. Food alleviates hunger, promotes well-being, and restores energy, but is it not, sometimes, out-of-date and contaminated, causing harm rather than good? Is there, then, anyone who would conclude, based on this possibility, that food is dangerous for the body? Everything, no matter how useful and beneficial it may be, becomes harmful if it is placed in the wrong hands or if it is used incorrectly. Thus, one needs only to be cautious not to use anything in the wrong way. The improper use of the principle of testimony is to accept a fabricated and unreliable testimony as the basis of a decision. If we safeguard ourselves against this improper application, testimony is an extremely useful and reliable means of acquiring knowledge; no wise person can deny this.

When we review the doctrine of the existence of God according to the above-mentioned principle, the doctrine appears to be established on the basis of the strongest testimony in the world. Every Prophet or Messenger who appeared in the world, regardless of his country, era, or nation, bore witness that there is a God who is the Creator and Master and Governor of this universe. They do not say so on the basis of conjecture or hearsay, but claim that they have seen and recognised God, just as they see and recognise other non-material things. They claim to have a personal bond with God and are as certain about His existence as they are certain about the existence of their father, brother, friend, town, and home. They claim that God converses with them, listens to them, answers them, and helps them when they are in need. In short, all the Prophets and Messengers bear witness in most clearly defined and unambiguous words that there is a God who is the Creator and Master of this universe. As stated above, their testimony is not based on hearsay but on their personal experience and observation and is not limited to any one country, people or age; indeed, such testimony is found in every country among every people and has been given in every age. Ādam[as], Nūḥ[as] [Noah], Yūnus[as] [Jonah] and Ayyūb[as] [Job], Ibrāhīm[as] [Abraham] and Lūṭ[as] [Lot], Ismā'īl[as] [Ishmael] and Isḥāq[as] [Isaac], Ya'qūb[as] [Jacob] and Yūsuf[as] [Joseph], Mūsā[as], [Moses] and Hārūn[as] [Aaron], Dāwūd[as] [David] and Suleimān[as] [Solomon], Zakariyyā[as] [Zachariah] and Yaḥyā[as] [John], all bear witness to it. Masīḥ [the Messiah] of Nazareth bears witness to it. Zartasht [Zoroaster], Confucius, Krishan, and Ramachandra bear witness to it. Ḥaḍrat Muhammad Muṣṭafā [the Chosen One], peace and blessings of Allah be on him, bears witness to it. In this age, the Promised Messiah, may peace be on him, bears witness to it. Moreover, all of the Founders of religions, who have come and gone, have presented their personal testimonies that this universe is subservient to an Omnipotent and Possessive God, who is the Creator and Master, and nothing is outside His authority. These are people whose truthfulness, honesty, and integrity is accepted by friends and foes. Even the enemies, who may not accept their faith, acclaimed their righteousness and truthfulness. These Prophets were not insane, inadequate, or fanatics; indeed, they were granted the best abilities of hearts and minds. Therefore, their testimony should be regarded as beyond contention and most powerful.

My dear ones! Think hard. Various people are born in different parts of the world, among different nations at different times. Their truthfulness, honesty, and integrity are beyond reproach. Their sanity is unquestionable; they are regarded as models for others on account of their outstanding truthfulness and exalted mental faculties. They are not ten, twenty, fifty, or a hundred, but number in the thousands, and are spread over different countries and different ages. They all present their personal testimony to the world that this universe and all therein is under the authority and governance of an Exalted Being. They testify that they have seen and perceived Him as they see and perceive other non-material things. They say they have a connection with Him as they have with other perceived and observed things. Is this testimony not worthy of acceptance? If this testimony is not acceptable, then surely there can be no other testimony in the world which would be found acceptable.

Only two factors can create doubt about a testimony. First, if the truthfulness of the witness is in question. Second, if the witness is unreliable, for he may not lie deliberately, but may err in his observation and experience. This is not the case with Prophets; indeed, they are regarded in the highest esteem for their truthfulness and intellectual abilities. Their evidence is not based on hearsay, but on their own personal and witnessed accounts. They lived in different ages among different nations and most of them were not even aware of the presence of other Prophets and, therefore, could not be suspected of conspiracy. Under these circumstances, their testimony is so weighty that it cannot be ignored at all.

Consider this: A lawsuit is brought to you for judgement. On one side, there is a party comprising thousands of men—each one of them such that his truthfulness and sound-mindedness are admitted to by friend and foe alike. They all submit their eyewitness accounts individually, that they saw a particular person at a particular place. On the other side is a party comprising a mixed lot, and they state that they did not see the person. In which party's favour will you give your judgement? If you do not deem yourself competent enough to judge, consult one versed in law. Such a one will tell you that the testimony of those who undoubtedly witnessed a person is far superior, and forms the basis of the final judgement. Those who did not see anyone, no matter how many of these there be, will have no impact on the judgement. This is because it is possible for people to miss or not see something that is present; but it is not possible for a collection of wise and sensible people to see something that does not exist.

In short, the testimony presented by the Prophets and Messengers about the existence of God is extremely strong evidence that there indeed is a God. If we add the *Ṣulaḥā'* [Righteous ones] and the *Auliyā'* [Friends of Allah] of different nations of the world to the Prophets and Messengers, the testimony becomes so weighty that rejecting it amounts to insanity. Among the followers of each Prophet there have been hundreds of thousands of *Ṣulaḥā'* and *Auliyā'* who ruled the hearts of the people in their circles because of their righteousness, wisdom, and sagacity; their truthfulness, honesty, and integrity served as a model for the people. Like the Prophets, these people too bore witness that there is a God and the universe is operating under His governance. Their testimony is based not on hearsay but, like the Prophets, on their personal experience. Therefore, until it can be proven that millions of Prophets, *Ṣulaḥā'*, and *Auliyā'* who appeared in different ages among different people were, God forbid, liars or mad or dim-witted, their great testimony—that they have seen and recognised God and have a personal relationship with Him—will stand firm and cannot be challenged by atheists. Can an atheist summon the courage to venture forth to prove to the world that Ibrāhīm[as], Mūsā[as], 'Īsā[as], Krishan, and Zartasht were liars or insane; or the Holy Prophet[saw], the Promised Messiah, and, likewise, all other Prophets were liars or insane, not to mention all those innumerable Ṣulaḥā' and Auliyā' in every nation? No atheist can prove this. Is it not regrettable then that you believe in the existence of London, the North Pole, and the South Pole only on the say so of others; you believe the newspaper reports of other countries as related by Reuters, Havas, or some other news agency; and you accept new scientific facts as reported by the scientists without personally being involved in these experiments; but you reject the idea of the presence of God in the face of the testimony of millions of knowledgeable and righteous persons.

تِلْكَ اِذًا قِسْمَةٌ ضِيْزٰى ¹

One may argue, granted, I have not seen with my own eyes the things others claim [to have seen in existence], but the ability to see and observe those things is open to all. I would say: My dear naïve friends! May God grant you wisdom! The avenue for finding God is also open to you. Those who claim to have found God openly claim that if you adopt the path indicated by them—the path of reaching God—you, like them, can also find God and establish a

---

1. That indeed is an unfair division. (*Sūrah an-Najm*, 53:23) [Publisher]

connection with Him. This is not merely a claim; innumerable people have followed them and have indeed succeeded in attaining knowledge of God. Try, if you will. It is unfortunate that people accept that attainment of any worldly objective requires them to follow a certain method, without which the objective cannot be achieved—and that it takes time and effort—but for spiritual objectives, they hope to achieve results immediately just having wished for them! It can certainly not happen like that. And if you are wise and ponder over the matter, you will agree that this is not how it should happen. This is the truth. Accept, if you will. For achieving any purpose, be it material or spiritual, there is a definite methodology that must be followed. The greater and higher the objective, the greater the time, attention, hard work, sacrifices, and discipline it requires. But when it comes to God, you wish to find him without any effort on your part. By God, you will never find Him that way. If you tread along the path that leads to God with real eagerness, heartfelt desire, full attention, and exert due effort, and still do not find Him, then you have the right to claim that you sought Him but did not find Him. It is impossible that you should seek God the proper way but fail to find Him. Millions of men, human beings like you, who had hearts and minds like you, sought God and found Him. The history of the world records their testimony, personal and eyewitness accounts, in clear and unambiguous words. It is not possible for you to challenge their testimony. You cannot call them fraudsters, dim-witted, mad, or connivers. Thus, there is no reason to reject their testimony merely on the basis of your conjectures.

It could be suggested that they were not deceivers or dim-witted, but were themselves deceived, and anyone can be the victim of deception. Of course, even clever people can be deceived, but just because they can be deceived does not mean that they are indeed the victims of deception. This assertion can be credible only if backed up by concrete evidence proving that these people had in fact been involved in some mistake or deception. What is there in the world about which one cannot be deceived? Shall we then declare everything in the world doubtful? We will open the gate for superstition in such a way that nothing will remain certain. Therefore, the burden of proof lies with those who claim that all of these people, testifying to the existence of God, are victims of deception. Otherwise, it would be a childish attempt to refute the testimony of hundreds of thousands of righteous, intelligent personages and no wise man would take it seriously. Therefore, it is insane to turn down the testimony of hundreds of thousands of Prophets from all ages and all nations; they were recognised to be intelligent, righteous, and truthful individuals, who based their testimony on personal experience and not hearsay. To say that their testimony could be a mistaken one is irrational and would not be acceptable to any wise person.

Second, self-deception takes place in certain specific situations. An intelligent and sound-minded person may be deceived in matters relating only to opinions and ideas subject to argumentation. It is possible that two persons—both sound-minded—may differ on an academic issue, because there is a possibility of misconception in matters involving opinions and argumentation. However, for a sound-minded person with normal perception there is no possibility of deception in matters relating to observation, especially when it concerns something in which he is particularly interested. Accepting the possibility of deception in such a situation would open the gates of dangerous superstition; peace would vanish from the earth and no observation would remain certain. Can a sound-minded person deceive himself into taking a stranger for his long-standing friend, or into regarding an unknown person as his father or brother? Obviously, none other than a mad or confused person can fall into such an error.

When we look at the testimony of the Prophets and *Ṣulaḥāʾ* according to this principle, we have to accept their testimony to be beyond the possibility of self-deception, because they do not say that they have deduced God through logical arguments. They claim they have indeed found God and established a personal relationship with Him and that they speak with Him. He hears them and answers them and helps them with His mighty help when they are in need. They do not attribute their observation to a certain period of their lives, but claim to have spent the whole of their lives with that observation ever since they found God. That is to say, their observation spans many years uninterruptedly till their last breath. The practical consequences of their observation are also before the world. This being the case, no wise man can, therefore, think that they might have been mistaken. If we accept the possibility of misunderstanding in such circumstances, all sciences in the world would be reduced to conjecture. One may say that witnesses are mentally infirm, but having accepted them to be mentally sound, one cannot then turn around and call them self-deceived.

Third, this testimony is not from one person, not from people of one nation, not from people of one country, not from people of one age, but from hundreds of thousands of people spread over all countries, over all nations and through all ages. How many of them will you declare mistaken? One or two persons may be deluded, or people of a particular age or type could be misguided, but it is strange that hundreds of thousands of sound-minded people, in different nations, different ages, and different countries, generally unaware of each other, fell prey to it. Thus, the large number of witnesses—coming from every nation, every faith, every age, and every country, presenting their testimony individually and independently of each other—constitutes a strong argument that all of these wise people could not have been mistaken or misguided.

To summarise, millions of Prophets, *Auliyā*, and *Ṣulaḥā'* from all nations, all eras, and all parts of the world openly and independently proclaim that they have seen and recognised God. The world also accepts that they are not liars, pedlars, insane, or confused. Each one of them testifies separately and independently and their testimony is based not on hearsay but on their personal observation, spanning their entire life. This compels us to accept their testimony. We draw conclusions about testimonies that pertain to worldly matters based on our knowledge and judgement; therefore, the testimony of the Prophets is compelling—that this universe is subservient to one Creator and Master, an All-Knowing and Wise, Omnipotent and Governing Being and nothing is beyond His domain.

The Holy Quran has also presented this principle of testimony and has accordingly called the Prophets 'witnesses':

$$ اِنَّاۤ اَرْسَلْنَاۤ اِلَيْكُمْ رَسُوْلًا ۙ شَاهِدًا عَلَيْكُمْ كَمَاۤ اَرْسَلْنَاۤ اِلٰى فِرْعَوْنَ رَسُوْلًا ۚ ^1 $$

---

1. *Sūrah al-Muzzammil*, 73:16.

That is, O people! We have sent Muhammad, peace and blessings of Allah be on him, as a Messenger, to be a witness for you even as we sent Mūsā to Pharaoh as a witness.

By the Grace of Allah, I now conclude the logical arguments about the existence of God. I have also briefly responded to doubts that could arise. As I stated at the outset, I have avoided complicated and intricate discussions as much as possible and stated simple points in an easily understandable manner. I hope that a good-natured and sensible person, not given to raising unnecessary doubts, will be satisfied with my brief discourse concerning logical arguments. As I stated elsewhere in this treatise, true satisfaction and utmost certainty can be achieved only through personal experience and observation. For this, it is necessary to study the lives of the Prophets and the *Auliyā'* and follow their footsteps. I will, God willing, present a glimpse of that in due course.

GREAT BENEFITS OF
BELIEF IN GOD

Now, I would like to state some arguments for the existence of God, based on the principle that belief in God carries some important and exclusive benefits. We do things in this world based on their relative benefit and gain. We weigh the benefit of a certain action for human beings. If it is established that belief in God is good and advantageous for mankind, every wise man will agree, for this reason alone if nothing else, that the doctrine should not be rejected. These considerations do not argue for the existence of God—nor do they suggest that there ought to be one—but certainly indicate that the doctrine is useful for the progress and well-being of mankind and, as useful things should be adopted, these arguments can also be presented to indirectly support the existence of God. At the outset of my logical arguments, I suggested caution based on the precept that belief in God is not detrimental in any way, whereas denial may be and, therefore, it is safer to believe. Similarly, to conclude my logical arguments, I would suggest another type of circumspection that, because the doctrine of belief in God is useful and profitable, it is better and preferable to adopt it. But remember, we are not discussing here the great religious or spiritual benefits gained by belief in God, such as establishing a personal relationship with Him, gaining His support, increasing our knowledge and insight, and salvation in the Hereafter. We are simply discussing the basic benefits generally gained or that can be gained by mankind as a result of a logical belief in God, and only these will be mentioned here.

Belief in God Creates Unity and Brotherhood

The first benefit of belief in God that I would like to mention is that it creates the extremely useful sentiments of unity and brotherhood in the hearts of the people, which are essential for the progress and welfare of mankind. It is essential for world peace and welfare of the world's nations that they live with mutual love and brotherhood, and do not permit any prejudice to take root in their hearts. They should instead adopt the policy of sympathy, sacrifice, and selflessness for others to the best of their ability. Similarly, at the individual level it is also essential to develop the spirit of mutual love and brotherhood, sympathy, and cooperation. Without this spirit—which is essential both for individuals and nations—world peace, progress, and the welfare of mankind are impossible. Therefore, it is the duty of every well-wisher of mankind to pursue all of the means that create and nurture unity and mutual brotherhood, and prevent feelings of malice, jealousy, undue rivalry, and prejudice from taking root in the hearts.

As stated above, belief in God is the greatest and most effective means for that.

This doctrine—that, despite our numerous and multifarious differences, we are created by, and belong to, an Omnipotent and All-Governing Being with a decisive will who is our final refuge and shelter—creates uniquely strong and clear sentiments of mutual love, unity, and brotherhood in our hearts. Belonging to the same country, nation, governing authority, etc., creates unity and brotherhood to a variable extent. However, the most powerful motivator for this is the belief that we are the creation of one Creator and we originate from one fountainhead of Grace and that our Master is not like a deceased father whose undisciplined sons sometimes start quarrelling with one another after him, but He is very much alive and will remain alive forever. This belief puts the whole of mankind on equal footing, like brothers. With the inception of that belief, the sentiments of resentment, rancour, malice, and hostility to each other start vanishing and are replaced by sentiments of love, brotherhood, sympathy, and sacrifice. Belief in God is akin to regarding one another as the offspring of the same father and mother. Once you believe in God, you have to agree that the relationship of man with God is deep and vast, the like of which cannot be found among any worldly relations.

In short, belief in God is the strongest motive for creation of mutual love and brotherhood. Patriotic and nationalistic ideas also create these sentiments. But the impact of such ideas is not as strong or deep and tends to be limited to a certain group, rather than the whole of the human race. Moreover, on occasion it could be counterproductive, as it leads to sectarianism, nationalism, undue prejudice, and jealousy. It is only belief in God that can create the sentiments of unity and brotherhood in the human race worldwide. Take away the idea of God from people's hearts and the sentiments of unity and brotherhood will start vanishing instantaneously, leaving only legal and business dealings among the people, which can never produce any sentimental ties. Remember well that if there is no God and everyone is by himself and is independent, then there can be no unity or brotherhood. On the contrary, selfishness, undue rivalry, and jealousy would become rampant, and they are the greatest causes of strife in the world. It is only the idea of God and nothing else that can create brotherhood in the human race in certain and definite terms. Take away this belief and it would be impossible for this sentiment to last universally as a living reality.

I am not saying that everyone who claims to believe in God has sentiments of mutual brotherhood and unity. Many factors affect the state of man and it is possible that under the effect of other influences, a believer in God may not harbour these pious feelings. It is also possible that one's belief in God is too weak to create sentiments of brotherhood and unity in his heart and mind. However, in principle, belief in God is undoubtedly the most important and the greatest factor in creating such sentiments. In the absence of other factors, a believer in God is certainly more sympathetic, beneficent, and more loving towards mankind than a disbeliever. Everyone who earnestly believes in God will bear witness that belief in God keeps generating in him sentiments of brotherhood and unity very strongly, and that these sentiments influence his actions as well. One who is given to analysing himself will certainly realise that, God forbid, if belief in God is done away with, he will never be the same again. This belief creates a kind of love, tenderness, and affinity, not only between human beings, but also generates these same types of sentiments in one's heart for lower animals, plant life, and inanimate objects.

There is a saying: 'Love me, love my dog'. That is, if you love me, you must love everything about me. This saying is based on an accurate analysis of human nature. If we really believe in God and have a relationship with Him, then it is absolutely impossible that our heart be devoid of love for His creation—especially for man. I can accept that one who claims to believe in God may be false in his claim or self-deceived. But I cannot accept even for a moment that the heart of one who truly believes in God can be devoid of love and sympathy for creation (because that would be against human nature). The history of the world also bears witness to the fact that those who have a strong belief in God have a higher level of sympathy and love for mankind. When people's belief [in God] weakens, their sentiments of love and brotherhood also decline. In short, there is absolutely no doubt that belief in God is the strongest, surest, and fastest acting motive for unity and brotherhood among the human race. As the sentiments of unity and brotherhood are essential for world peace and desirable progress and welfare of all nations, every wise person is obligated not to abandon this useful and blessed belief.

One may think that those who do not believe in God commonly treat others with love and sympathy and take interest in philanthropic activities, indicating that belief in God is not essential for such sentiments. Our answer is that we never claimed that such sentiments cannot be produced by anything other than belief in God. We believe that many factors produce such sentiments to a variable extent. However, we maintain that only belief in God can produce these sentiments in their most perfect form and in a comprehensive manner in mankind. Other factors in their capacity and quantity cannot compare with it. Therefore, our claim can be rejected only if it can be proven logically that belief in God cannot motivate sentiments of brotherhood and love; or if it can be demonstrated by experience and observation that those who do not believe in God are more sympathetic, philanthropic, and loving to mankind than those who believe in Him. Unless either of the two is established, no one has the right to contend that belief in God is not, or atheism is, conducive to such sentiments, merely on the grounds that an atheist also has such sentiments to some extent.

I cannot believe that a sensible person can accept even for a moment that atheism in itself can—or that belief in God cannot—be conducive to these sentiments. These two statements are so obviously unnatural and contrary to *fiṭrah* that no sensible person can accept them. If properly believed in, God is the focal point upon which all creation ultimately converges. The concept of unity and oneness are inseparably linked to this focal point; rejecting it [i.e. God] is tantamount to admitting that this universe has no centre or origin. As soon as you entertain this notion, ideas of unity and oneness start vanishing. Can anyone say that common fatherhood cannot lead to unity and brotherhood but separate fatherhood can? No, never! If, at times, sons of different fathers live together in peace and with love, we cannot conclude that common fatherhood cannot lead to love and brotherhood. We will instead infer that some other factors have brought them together at one point despite, but not because of, being sons of different fathers. Likewise, admittedly, if these sons of different fathers—strung together in unity and oneness by some factors despite this difference—were in fact sons of the same father, their mutual love and brotherhood would express itself more perfectly. Therefore, if atheists at times are found to be loving and sympathetic to other humans, this does not mean that belief in God is not needed anymore. These sentiments would manifest only in their perfect form, quantitatively and qualitatively, when, in addition to other motives for unity, people are united in their belief in God—when they regard themselves as originating from one source of creation and springing forth from one fountain of life.

My dear ones! How can I convince you that belief in God (if it is a real and living belief) stirs up a vast ocean of love and sympathy for mankind and sentiments of brotherhood for them? It is impossible to find a parallel elsewhere. All other motives for such sentiments are empty rhetoric by comparison, both quantitatively and qualitatively.

If the question is asked, why does an atheist have these sentiments, there are generally two reasons. First, consciously or subconsciously, an atheist, influenced by teachings of religions in his environment, concludes that [expressing] sympathy and love for mankind is a good deed and not doing this will lower his standing among people. In addition to losing respect personally, he feels that he will give the people a chance to criticise his beliefs, saying that he lacks sentiments of love and brotherhood for mankind because he is an atheist. Therefore, intentionally or unintentionally, he tries not to lag behind those who believe in God in those deeds that are universally considered to be good. In other words, the spirit of competition and fear of disrepute motivate him to these acts. Obviously, these sentiments cannot find highest and most perfect expression in him and will never acquire the selfless and natural character found in one who believes in God. His love is like that of a stepmother, who shows love for the children of her husband's deceased wife to please her husband or to guard against disrepute in the neighbourhood. But the people can tell the difference between a mother's instinctive love that surges naturally in her bosom, and a stepmother's pretensions—with perhaps rare exceptions. Second, like others, an atheist also realises that it is essential for the progress and welfare of mankind and the stability of social order that people live with mutual love and harmony and cooperate with each other in matters that promote physical, moral, intellectual, and economic welfare of the people. Therefore, an atheist, being a citizen of the world, develops such sentiments and takes an interest in such matters. Obviously, this state of affairs has a legal and business character and cannot produce the natural and sentimental ties produced by belief in God. A person who develops sentiments of sympathy for mankind for such reasons cannot attain the status of a person who has developed love and brotherhood for mankind because, considering that they are creation of one God, this passion has become part of his nature. In other words, whereas belief in God creates these sentiments in one's heart in a natural way, the ideas that come from reflection draw one's attention to it only in legal and business terms. The difference is obvious.

To summarise, the motives that arouse sympathy for mankind in an atheist can never lead him to the high level of nobility, attainable as a result of belief in God. Moreover, it should be remembered that other motives that arouse sympathy and love are general, from which a believer in God can benefit as well as an atheist. However, the sentiments created by belief in God are specific to the believers and an atheist cannot derive benefit from them. It is obvious when several factors exert their influence collectively, the result will definitely be more perfect. Therefore, belief in God emerges as beneficial and profitable from this point of view as well.

It should also be remembered that although all other motives of unity may produce—to some extent—the spirit of cooperation, sympathy, and sacrifice, they cannot produce the sentiment of brotherhood, for this can only develop if one Creator, Master, and Lord of mankind is acknowledged. Brotherhood implies that all of us originated from one source. However much cooperation or sympathy other motives may produce among individuals or nations, they can never produce brotherhood. From this point of view as well, the need for belief in God and its usefulness is established. It is obvious that unless sentiments of brotherhood and unity are born naturally in the human race, their apparent unity and cooperation cannot be such as can attain any reliable status. There will always be a danger of minor disputes stirring up selfishness and creating rancour and hostility. World peace will remain severely endangered unless and until people establish this belief as a living reality—that there is one God, who is our Creator and Master. Therefore, we should live like brothers and should not act unjustly in the face of a conflict; rather, we should be prepared to act selflessly and make sacrifices for each other. In fact, if one ponders carefully, it will be seen that legal and business ties are based on selfishness, because one knows that not investing in a good relationship with others would result in others doing the same, and this may affects one's personal interests. Therefore, one adopts the policy of good behaviour as a safety measure and treats others with sympathy and cooperation, expecting them to reciprocate accordingly. Although the effect is useful and profitable to some extent, it cannot compare with the lofty and noble station wherein sentiments of brotherhood and unity are developed as natural feelings. That natural feeling which unfolds itself in the form of brotherhood can never be achieved without belief in God.

Is Religion the Cause of War and Disorder in the World?

Before going any further, it is essential to dispel one doubt created by some, that religion causes war, conflict, and sectarian divides. It is alleged that religion leads to a narrow-mindedness and lack of fortitude that has disastrous implications for world peace, as well as the progress and welfare of mankind. Therefore, they suggest that people should abandon religion to develop tolerance and broad-mindedness that will enable them to live harmoniously with each other, promoting peace and mutual love. As religion originates from the concept of God, it is argued that a god who is the cause of conflict and strife in this world should be forsaken. This is the objection raised by people with a modern education and greatly promoted by European philosophers. Evidently, this objection is based on a lack of deliberation. However, before I come to the actual answer, I would say that even if we accept the validity of this objection—i.e. admit that religion does cause what has been stated—it cannot serve as an argument against the existence of

God. That is to say, it cannot prove that there is no Creator of this universe. At the most, it can prove that belief in God leads to narrow-mindedness and a violation of peace. However, if God does exist, then, whatever the consequences of believing in Him, we have no right to deny His existence. Therefore, if the existence of God is established, we cannot deny it even if religion causes strife. But in reality it is absolutely incorrect that religion causes disorder, and those who believe this have made a grave mistake.

Above, we established that belief in God creates sentiments of mutual love and brotherhood naturally and instinctively. Belief in God eliminates all national and racial prejudices and creates a worldwide brotherhood. Without belief in God, worldwide brotherhood is inconceivable. How, then, can belief in God lead to strife and narrow-mindedness? Strife and narrow-mindedness have no connection at all with the concept of God. Logically, it is unacceptable that the concept of God—not a national or racial God, but the Creator and Master of the whole of mankind— should manifest in the form of narrow-mindedness, national prejudices, strife, and sectarian divide. No sane person can find a cause-and-effect relationship between the two. Thus, if religions do lead to disorder, narrow-mindedness, and national prejudice, we should look for its cause elsewhere and try to find out why this happens, rather than attributing it unjustly and unnaturally to belief in God.

Unfortunately, those who make this criticism have witnessed religions in a state where religion exists in name alone. This objection is specific to the present age and, unfortunately, the followers of all faiths are far removed from the essence of their religions. There is not a single religion whose followers truly adhere to its teachings. Instead, the teachings of religions have been corrupted by the actions of humans, giving an opportunity to free-minded individuals to raise objections against religions. But the fact of the matter is that, of all means that promote world peace and enlightened minds, religion is the most powerful one. Whenever people adhered to the essence of religion, it decreased discord and undue strife and promoted broad-mindedness and fortitude. A study of religious history demonstrates that during periods when the followers of any particular religion abided by its teachings, they were found to be magnanimous, broad-minded, sympathetic, and seekers of peace and reconciliation. In contrast, during the age when these followers gave up their teachings and their commitment to religions existed in name only, they became narrow-minded, lacking in fortitude, prejudiced, petulant, and anarchistic. I make this claim without fear of contradiction and for every religion, and I believe anyone who researches history honestly in this matter will reach the same conclusion. By the Grace of Allah, I am a Muslim and take the greatest pride in counting myself among the humblest servants of the Holy Prophet[saw]. Nevertheless, I cannot but make the regrettable admission that, these days, like other people, the Muslims are also afflicted by the dangerous and disastrous ill that is called narrow-mindedness. Undue national prejudices have overcome their sublime and noble sentiments. Quarrelsomeness and inclination to violation of peace over petty differences have permeated their nature. Is Islam to blame for this? No, never! These things did not exist among the Muslims when they followed the true teachings of Islam and the Islamic spirit was alive in them. They were a nation of bright-minded and big-hearted people; they were well-wishers and sympathisers of mankind, peace-loving and selfless, and made sacrifices for others. They illumined the whole world with rays of their universal light. What we see today are the ruins of that magnificent edifice!

The same applies to other nations. Early Christians were a very good model of self-sacrifice and sympathy for mankind; they sought peace and conciliation. However, once the Christians moved away from the real teachings and spirit of Christianity, they exceeded in injustice, tyranny, bloodshed, and religious prejudices. History bears witness to the narrow-mindedness, undue prejudices, strife, murder, and pillage displayed by the so-called followers of Ḥaḍrat Masīḥ [i.e. Jesus the Messiah], may peace be on him, during the Reformation.

The history of Hinduism, Sikhism, and other religions reveals more or less the same pattern; even more horrendously so among the Hindus and Sikhs. All of this proves that in reality the blame does not lie with religion but with those who forsake the essence of their religion. Unfortunately, all the nations of the world have lost the spirit of religion, giving the impetuous and short-sighted critics an opportunity to blame religion for [their] narrow-mindedness and violence.

That is why God—who is Holy, who does not like to see the world immersed in the darkness of ignorance, out of His loving Kindness and Grace—commissioned one of His righteous servants, Ḥaḍrat Mirza Ghulam Ahmad of Qadian, the Promised Messiah and Imam Mahdi, for the guidance of mankind in this age, so that he could answer the allegations raised against religion because of the misdeeds of its followers. These misdeeds distant humans from God and promote violence, coercion, and narrow-mindedness in the context of religion. The Promised

Messiah[as] was sent so that the people recognise their heavenly Master and Lord and become like brothers again. Regrettably, as is typical of these people, they treat the servants of this divine reformer and torch bearers of this heavenly guidance with ignorance. Several innocent Ahmadis were most cruelly stoned to death in Kabul only because they were Ahmadis. Thus, giving others the opportunity to raise objections against Islam that it promotes violence, coercion, intolerance, prejudice, and tyranny. Alas! How very aptly a poet has said:

من از بیگانگاں هرگز نہ نالم   کہ با من هر چہ کرد آں آشنا کرد

I certainly do not complain about the strangers,
Because all that was done to me was done by those who knew me.

To summarise, the notion that religion is the cause of intolerance and discord arises from the condition that prevails currently. A study of world history makes it absolutely clear that when the people adhere to the real spirit and essence of religion, they develop broad-mindedness, enlightenment, peacefulness, self-sacrifice, and tolerance more than others. As regards to the teachings, without going into details, there is no religion that does not teach peace, conciliation, and tolerance in principle. Therefore, narrow-mindedness and conflict may result from forgetting the teaching but certainly not from abiding by it.

Second, let me dispel another doubt. If carefully contemplated, it is logically impossible that a person who understands the reality and objective of religion would perpetrate narrow-mindedness or trouble. Religion is not like a country or a nation that is confined by geographical boundaries or national limits and cannot be expanded. On the contrary, religion comprises doctrines, notions and a code of conduct pertaining to obligations to God and obligations to mankind; one accepts religion as truth and endeavours to disseminate it to others. Religion is like a building with its doors open for everyone, regardless of his nation or country; rather, every religious person invites others to this building. So anyone, who truly aims to fulfil the object of religion, can never perpetrate narrow-mindedness or strife. On the contrary, he will try his best to win others over with high morals and peaceful preaching, avoiding anything that may become a barrier for others to accept religion. Therefore, it is absolutely impossible for one to commit intolerance and conflict after grasping the essence and objective of religion.

Third, if at times religion leads to conflict and war, do other factors not also cause strife? There are many causes of conflict and war between individuals and nations, should these all be abandoned for this reason? There are dozens of factors like national and political differences, national interests, business and economic matters, etc., that lead to conflict and war between nations of the world. Likewise, undeniably there are hundreds of causes of discord between individuals. Will all these be forsaken just because at times they lead to disturbance of peace? If yes, then everyone should give up everything in life and become a recluse to avoid interacting with others and thus avoid all possibilities of conflict and discord.

Look at the history of world. Religious difference was certainly not the cause of most of the wars that took place. They were caused by national or political differences, national interests, economic and business matters, and at times by other factors. There was absolutely no religious factor involved in the last World War. All the bloodshed—unparalleled in its scope and devastation in the history of the world—was caused only by political motives. So give up politics as it leads to war at times.

My dear ones! This is all due to lack of knowledge and ignorance. There is no particular association between religion and intolerance, war, or strife. However, like all other causes of breaches of the peace, on relatively few occasions, religion can be used to create discord, but only in those circumstances where people have forgotten the true teachings of their religion. For instance, during the time of the Holy Prophet[saw] the Jews and the idolaters waged a war of aggression and injustice against the inno- cent Muslims because they misunderstood the true teachings of their religion. Then, Muslims had to react in self-defence. This led to a state of war which was entirely brought on by the idolaters and Jews, who did not grasp the reality and object of religion. The Muslims engaged in this war only to establish peace.

In short, it is absolutely absurd and nonsensical to think that religion causes war and strife. In fact, religion is the only force that can effectively end strife and it is the defiance of the essence of reli- gion that causes breach of peace and conflict. Even if, as a remote possibility, we were to accept that religious differences lead to war and strife, the objectors have no right to turn away from religion inasmuch as there are many other factors that lead to breach of peace and strife and no sensible person gives them up for this rea- son. The fact of the matter is that any dispute, if handled badly, will lead to regretful consequences; this is by no means unique to religion. Poor handling of political, national, commercial, and economic differences leads to war. Likewise, improper application of religious differences can also lead to war. The only difference is that, whereas improper application of other factors leads to breach of peace, their proper application does not particularly lead to peace, cooperation, and brotherhood. However, religion in its original form and practised properly, particularly leads to peace, cooperation, unity, brotherhood, and sympathy. That is the truth. Accept it, if you will.

Fourth, critics have misunderstood the term 'religion'. They probably think that religion implies only belief in God, and when one gives up that belief he has, as it were, given up religion. In other words, they think religion is something that one can give up. However, while one who gives up belief in God is technically termed 'irreligious', religion is an essential part of human life and it is impossible to completely break out of its confines. Religion, in fact, is the name of beliefs, doctrines, and codes of conduct one adopts about life and death. Obviously, in this sense, it is logically impossible for one to part with religion inasmuch as everyone adopts a certain way of life. One can say that he does not like this religion or that religion but it is impossible to be completely independent of religion. As long as one is living, he must hold some beliefs concerning life and death and must follow a code of conduct. The sum total of his beliefs and code of conduct would be called his religion. At most, one may separate himself from known revealed religions and invent a new religion for himself. However, he cannot really be labelled as not having a religion according to the definition given above. Whatever way of life he adopts will be his religion. If someone believes in God, that is his religion, and if he denies Him, that is his religion. In short, religion is composed of the way of life and beliefs that one adopts, and in that sense it is impossible to break away from religion. You can break away from Islam. You can break away from Christianity. You can break away from Hinduism. You can break away from Buddhism. You can break away from every other known revealed religion, but you cannot completely break away from religion. You will have to adopt a religion, even if invented by yourself. You will either believe in God or deny Him. If you believe in Him, you will have to acknowledge some attributes for Him. If you deny Him, you will have to postulate some doctrine concerning the genesis of this universe and beginning of life. You will have to adopt a code of conduct in dealings with friends, foes, relatives, non-relatives, husbands, wives, servants, masters, kings, the public, etc. Such doctrines and codes of conduct, or way of life, will constitute your religion. In short, religion is inseparably linked with life and no one can break out of the confines of religion. When someone is labelled 'pagan', it implies only that he is not following any of the known revealed religions, but has invented his own religion. Otherwise, no one can really be without a religion.

Obviously, when it is impossible to break out of the confines of religion, the suggestion—that because religion creates strife and narrow-mindedness one should break away from it—becomes absurd and ridiculous, and unbecoming of a sensible person. If by that, one implies breaking away from a known revealed religion, it would be ignorance. We are not speaking of a particular religion, rather religion in general causing war. If a particular religion does lead to conflict and breach of peace, we do not advocate it. We assert only that it is incorrect that religion is the cause of conflict and war, and even if it is, we cannot break away from it. Therefore, the suggestion of breaking away from religion is absurd.

Moreover, as a remote possibility, even if the people break away from the revealed religions, religious ideas will persist, because it is unlikely that, after breaking away from these religions, all of them will adopt an identical set of beliefs and code of conduct. In this case, the number of religions in the world will far exceed the current number. If there are currently ten to twenty religions, the number will multiply to thousands, even millions, as everyone would wish to invent a religion of his choice. This increase in number of religions will lead to an extraordinary multiplication of differences and consequent increase in conflict and bloodshed in the name of religion, from an occasional to everyday occurrence.

One might say that it is only the revealed religions—with doctrines of God, resurrection, and the Day of Judgement as the central themes—that can cause conflict and bigotry. This is because followers of each of these religions consider themselves as those who have achieved salvation and regard others destined for hell; this leads to mutual enmity and rivalry, whereas non-revealed, man-made religions not based on the notion of God and the Day of Judgement cannot cause such negative feelings. But this view is against human nature. Human nature triggers a feeling of compassion on seeing someone in danger and creates a desire to save them—that is the natural reaction. It is unnatural to feel hatred and contempt in this situation. Therefore, if followers of different sects regard themselves saved and the others lost, then their natural response should be of compassion and a desire to save them. Hatred and contempt are out of the question here. It is inconceivable that one would develop feelings of contempt and hatred for a drowning man; the natural instinct is to jump in the water in an attempt to save him. If someone, despite having the capacity, does not make an effort to save a drowning person, takes pleasure in seeing him in trouble and contemplates to harm him even more, he would be regarded as a fallen man with a dead conscience.

It is unnatural for a person to deride and undermine the followers of other religions if he truly believes that his own faith is the means of salvation. Such actions are against the essence of faith. We observe that only those who do not comprehend the true reality and lack the spirit of religion act in this improper manner. Those who comprehend the reality of religion empathise with those on the wrong path and do their best to save them from total destruction. It is not possible for men of true faith to even feel an iota of hatred and animosity for others.

Moreover, religious blessings and bounties are not like material goods, and those who share these are not afraid of losing them. On the contrary, these blessings and bounties are enhanced by sharing; hence, a religious person always seeks to share the blessings of his religion with others by inviting them to accept it. Thus, it is out of question to despise followers of other religions for the fear that they may lessen one's bounties.

To summarise, however we look at it, belief in God and affiliation to a religion can never lead to intolerance and conflict. If a 'religious' person, claiming to believe in God, creates narrow-mindedness and strife, lacks sentiments of sympathy and love for mankind, and instead entertains rancour and enmity towards them, and is mean-spirited and niggardly, he can never be labelled 'religious' in the real sense of the word. He is devoid of the holy spirit of religion, like a ruined house abandoned by its inhabitants. His claim to belief in God is a meaningless assertion. Unfortunately, such worthless persons abound in every faith these days and Islam is no exception, and this provides the critics with a justification to criticise Islam. However, a truly religious person who understands the philosophy of religion can never be malevolent and cause conflict.

Admittedly, people may at times suffer at the hands of a true believer in God. Nonetheless, that pain is akin to the discomfort of a bitter medication or apparently severe restrictions prescribed by a caring doctor. A religious person does sometimes take part in a war and brings about the killing of some, but this act is like that of a compassionate surgeon who amputates a man's limb to save his endangered life. Thus, he sacrifices something of comparatively little value to save something of greater value. Such an act is regarded as commendable by all wise men.

My dear ones! How can I convince you that when the Messengers of God and pious people declare war against anyone, they do so with the purest and most virtuous intention? Their hearts, like a brimming fountain, are always full of love and compassion for mankind. This is the living and eternal truth; testified to by God's pious people in every era. Would that you could understand!

An Interim Statement

Before proceeding any further, I would like to mention in passing that I began this treatise in June 1925 at Qadian. I wrote the first part during that summer at Mansuri, where I had to go on medical advice. When I returned to Qadian, I wrote the remaining part, in late 1925 and 1926. Because of certain circumstances—the burden of new responsibilities—the treatise remained incomplete till now; i.e. October 1927. It has occurred to me, and some of my friends have also suggested, that whatever portion has been written down should be published without awaiting its completion. I will, therefore, conclude the current discussion on the logical arguments about the existence of God in the next few pages and hand over the manuscript to the publisher. I pray to God that this book may be instrumental in guiding and reforming the people and that He may grant me the good fortune of completing the book. *Āmīn*. I had actually intended to address all of the questions pertaining to the Being and attributes of God, the Holy, including the logical arguments and testimonies for His existence, His attributes, the benefits and means of establishing a relationship with Him, and the distinguishing features of such a relationship. However, as readers might have noticed, I have not yet completed even the first part of the first question pertaining to logical arguments. Regrettably, of the five questions, not even half of the first has been dealt with, leaving the more important and essential part of the discussion untouched. I present to the readers that which has been written and pray to God for the remainder. If He so wills, He may make this much conducive for the guidance of people.

Belief in God Stops One from Committing Evil

The second major advantage of belief in God that benefits the entire world is that it stops one from committing evil acts. By and large, one refrains from sin and crime for three reasons. First, one might believe that by not committing evil, one would gain some benefits or reward. Second, one might fear the consequences or punishment as a result of committing some evil act. Third, because of one's enhanced knowledge and insight, one refrains from evil for the sake of it being evil.

There are no other factors stopping one from sin and crime. Out of the three factors, the third relates to the select few and the common people are not influenced by it. Though a believer has an edge over a non-believer in benefiting from the third, belief in God obviously also plays a major role in the other two factors. Whosoever believes in God also believes that evil deeds will displease God with consequent suffering and punishment, and abstaining from evil will please God with consequent benefits and rewards. Thus a person who really believes in God is more secure from sin than others. It is impossible for one believing in God to daringly commit evil. On the contrary, the more one advances in perfection of his belief the further he distances himself from sin and crime and disdains them.

Moreover, belief in God stops one from evil also because a believer regards God as Omnipresent and Knower of Unseen. Therefore, if a person possesses true faith, which is not pretentious or merely inherited, then the idea that God is watching over him will stop him from evil deeds. Indeed, it is not possible that every person is watched by a policeman all the time; that is why even the most powerful and strict governments have not been able to fully eradicate crime. It is only belief in God that can vigilantly guard over every heart all the time. One who earnestly believes in God cannot boldly embark on sin. Indeed, if such a person happens to commit a sin inadvertently, his faith will make him remorseful and will urge him to remain vigilant in the future. Therefore, belief in God is a definite and certain way to stop sin and crime, which is a great benefit the world can gain and, indeed, has always gained from it.

One may point out that those who believe in God also commit sin. Indeed, some of them do so at times. If looked carefully, these are the people who are weak and less-committed to their faith; their faith is based on the family they are born in and they have not cultivated the true spirit of faith. By and large, those who truly believe are definitely more protected from sin. Even if on occasion they stumble, this tends to be only a temporary phase and they promptly recover and become vigilant. This is further evidence that belief in God deters one from sin. Otherwise, what could explain why those with strong faith shun evil more frequently than those with weak faith. If all else is equal, it is seen the more that people advance in their faith and understanding, the more they are free of sin. Thus, this is an undeniable reality, proven throughout the ages, that a true faith in God is an effective means of eliminating sin from this world. This discussion can be elaborated further, but because of constraints of time and space I would be content with this much only.

Belief in God Promotes Good

The third major benefit of belief in God is that it inspires people to do good deeds. This can be established by similar arguments as mentioned above. For the sake of brevity, I shall not elaborate further.

Belief in God Helps in Study of the Reality of Things

The fourth major benefit of belief in God is that it enhances the capacity to research the reality of things. Indeed, those who believe that this world has come into existence by mere chance and follow the concept of random evolution can never be inspired to search the reality of matters and laws of nature with the same zeal and anticipation as those who are believers in God. A believer in God is totally convinced that everything in the world is created by God for a definite purpose. Nothing in the world is pointless, and everything in this universe undertakes the task entrusted to it in order to fulfil the purpose of its creation. Indeed, such a conviction inspires one tremendously to search the reality of this universe, stimulating great intellectual progress. By contrast, one who denies God and believes that this world has come into existence by some chance can never engage in the study of the reality of things with the same enthusiasm and expectation, for he subscribes to the possibility of mere chance and random transformations leading to the creation of things. Even if he does start his research for the sake of increasing his knowledge, he can never pursue it with the same perseverance and commitment of a believer. At every setback, he will be inclined to give up, thinking that there might not be anything worth discovering. A believer, on the other hand, will never waver in his belief that there is specific wisdom and a purpose behind everything and that God did not create anything in vain. He will, therefore, attribute his failures to lack of effort or error in his approach and will never give up.

It is a manifest reality that belief in God strongly motivates one to study the reality of things. One may question that in practice we observe that belief in God does not separate those who are interested in research in scientific matters or not; those who believe in God and those who do not are all interested in scientific research in the same manner. Rather, there are greater numbers of scientific researchers in Europe and America where atheism is more prevalent than in the East. However, this is a basic misconception, for the people in Europe and America are not atheists by religion. Indeed, they believe in God. No matter how weak their faith is, they solemnly affirm that everything has been created by God. Therefore, their superiority in understanding of the reality of things cannot form a basis for criticism. In the absence of relevant figures, one cannot comment on the claim that there are relatively more atheists in the West. It is possible that there are more atheists in the East than in the West but, unless something is established, no claim can be based on it.

Moreover, as Western nations are more advanced in worldly matters, their personal and national views are noticed readily, whereas, because of a lack of education, the personal views of the Eastern nations are barely presented to the world. In concordance with human psychology, it is possible that some Eastern people may not be fully aware of their own deeper views as they are not used to self-reflection because of a lack of education. They may be influenced by atheistic ideology, but may not be fully aware of this. But in Europe and America, the people, being well-educated, are used to self-reflection and can recognise any changes in their ideology. Therefore, it is quite possible that in the West there may be fewer atheists than it appears, and in the East there may be more atheists than we can see. Therefore, unless it is established that the atheists in the West outnumber those in the East, this objection is meaningless. Even if we assume that there are more atheists in the West, there would still be no room for objection, because history tells us that atheistic views originated in the West after the beginning of their progress in the acquisition of knowledge. The most we can infer from this is that this increase in knowledge inclined people to atheism and not that atheism inspired the West to academic progress. We cannot infer that disbelief in God inspires quest for knowledge more than belief in God does. In any case, the objection stands invalid.

Why, one may ask, has academic progress led to atheism? We do not accept that academic progress necessarily leads to or encourages atheism. The truth of the matter is that people have mistakenly drawn an utterly wrong conclusion. The fact is that progress in knowledge brings about awareness and replaces the inertia of ignorance with the energy of life. At such time, some misguided people, and those who are easily influenced by others and are confused, end up on the wrong path; whereas those stuck in ignorance stay put, because they do not have any opportunities to go astray. A poet has aptly put it:

گرتے ہیں شہسوار ہی میدانِ جنگ میں   وہ طفل کیا گرے گا جو گھٹنوں کے بل چلے

It is only the horsemen who fall in the battlefield;
   The baby who crawls on the knees cannot fall

This is not to say that one falls because of riding the horse. It means that a rider is exposed to a greater risk of falling and so, at times, he can fall from the horse. Thus, the greater influence of atheism in Western nations may be a reflection of education that has enlightened their minds. The enhanced curiosity of Western nations had motivated them to explore further; and in this quest some of them may go astray and stumble. Clearly, education is not to blame here, rather the incorrect application of education—an inevitable consequence of any pursuit of knowledge. Conversely, the nations that remain ignorant miss out on the benefits of education, but are also saved from the grave consequences of inappropriate application of this knowledge. That is the state of the East compared to the West. Nonetheless, it is inappropriate to present the state of affairs in the West to counter our argument.

So, to answer the question, 'Why are some atheists interested in study of the reality of matters?', well, we never claimed that such interest is created by belief in God only and nothing else. We admit that there are many factors that can create such interest and inclination. Therefore, it would not be objectionable at all if an atheist is motivated to study the universe by other factors. We only claim that belief in God is particularly helpful in the study of the reality of things. Other factors remaining equal, a believer will be more enthusiastic, more eager, more hopeful, more committed, and more spirited than a non-believer in the study of nature. That is because he believes that everything in this world is created with a purpose—something that an atheist does not believe. This is an undeniable truth.

Belief in God Brings about Satisfaction of the Heart

The fifth great benefit of belief in God is that it brings about a thorough peace of mind, which is useful in every walk of life.

In fact, one cannot do justice to anything unless he is at peace with himself. An atheist is always bedevilled with dissatisfaction, disquiet, and doubt and is never satisfied with his condition—unlike if he were wise and religiously inclined. He keeps wondering what if his findings are wrong and the universe did have a Creator and Master. Atheism is, in fact, a negative philosophy and is not based on any positive evidence. That is to say, an atheist is not in a position to claim that he has the categorical evidence that there is no God. All that he can say is that he has found no evidence that there is a God. The concept of atheism is in disagreement with the deepest philosophies of human nature; this is why he always harbours some doubts about his belief. His very own nature, his enlightened mind, and his surroundings all contribute to him feeling confused, vexed, and worried. Consequently, his quest for peace is never accomplished in this world.

Belief in God, on the other hand, is established on a strong positive basis and human nature finds comfort in it. Therefore, a believer in God is relatively more certain and resolute; he is not perturbed by the worries of the future and this peace of mind helps in all aspects of his life. Moreover, an atheist does have a deep down concern that if there is God, that he is disadvantaged by not believing in Him. Conversely, the possibility that there may not be a God does not disturb a believer as he would have nothing to lose. In short, whichever way you look at it, belief in God leads to peace of mind and disbelief to discontent, anxiety, and uncertainty. The Holy Quran says:

اَلَا بِذِكْرِ اللهِ تَطْمَئِنُّ الْقُلُوبُ [1]

Hearken, ye people! It is only in the concept and remembrance of Allah that hearts find comfort.

Peace of mind is an essential prerequisite for every task and nothing can be accomplished without it. We can, therefore, affirm that belief in God plays a major role in the progress and welfare of the world.

Belief in God Sets Moral Standards

The sixth major benefit of the belief in God is that it sets moral standards. Moral standards cannot be set without belief in God. Ethicists understand how difficult it is to set moral standards. One is amazed at the gross disagreement on the definition of virtue and moral standards ethicists propose after lengthy debates and deliberations. One says something and another something else and all of them criticize everyone else. But when one looks at the end result, there is nothing. However, once we believe in God, it becomes obvious that, as man did not come about by himself, he need not work out his own moral standard and try to determine what is good for him. Having been created by a Higher Being, it stands to reason that he has no model worth following other than that Higher Being and no moral objective other than reflecting the attributes of his Creator and Master. The Holy Prophet[saw] himself, states:

---

1. *Sūrah ar-Raʿd,* 13:29.

تَخَلَّقُوا بِاَخْلَاقِ اللهِ

That is, O people! Model your morals on the attributes of Allah.

Islam teaches that Allah, the Exalted, created man in the image of His own attributes, and the seeds of all His attributes (except those that are specific to God) have been sown in human nature, albeit in smaller and limited form. To nurture these natural seeds, He reveals a code of conduct—the Shariah—to His pious people from time to time. Shariah is the moral code that creates real reformation and progress in the world. Searching for an alternative is a wasted effort.

No proper moral standard can be established unless it proposes acquiring the attributes of the Creator and Master. In practical terms, it requires natural instincts—which argue for the existence of God, inasmuch as they reflect Divine attributes—be used properly, according to the Shariah, to take on Divine colours. For instance, love, loyalty, mercy, anger, and a sense of self-respect and honour are all natural instincts and when exercised properly they become high moral qualities. Likewise, there are many natural instincts that when exercised properly become high moral qualities. All these instincts are instilled in human nature as an image of their Creator's attributes. These instincts are simply natural impulses and, in themselves, are neither good nor bad. It is their use that makes them one or the other. The criterion for their use being proper or improper is that these natural instincts be exercised in conformity with Divine attributes as manifested by the acts of God, meaning nature, and His Words, meaning the

Shariah. There is no other solution for this complicated problem. This is a great benefit derived from belief in God.

There are many other benefits, but I bring this discussion to a close here. However, I wish to make it clear, that I have only discussed such benefits as are generally obtained through belief in God. I have not gone into much greater spiritual, moral, and intellectual benefits a believer and Divine communities derive in their pursuit for nearness to God. These will be mentioned later, God willing. I wish to add further that I have not presented these general benefits of belief in God as evidence of existence of God. For if there were no God, then the argument that we should believe in Him simply because it is beneficial to do so would be meaningless. This discussion was only meant to emphasise that not only do we have a Creator and Master, but that believing in Him has benefits for mankind.

REFUTATION OF ARGUMENTS
SUPPORTING ATHEISM

I would now like to refute very briefly the arguments put forward by the atheists to support their belief. Many have been refuted above, inasmuch as wherever I have put forward the arguments for existence of God I have also dealt with the common objections raised by the critics. However, some aspects have not been discussed above, as they could not be included in any of the sections dealing with positive arguments. I shall now proceed to discuss those aspects and only allude to the rest to complete the compilation.

Three Kinds of Atheists

It should be realised that there are three kinds of atheists:

First, there are those who believe that the existence of God is not established; i.e. they do not believe in God because they have no strong and convincing evidence to prove His existence. Such atheists are the majority and I think that more than 90% of the atheists fall in this category.

Second, there are those who hold the belief that existence of God can neither be proved nor disproved and, therefore, the issue cannot be resolved with arguments. For all practical purposes, these people too do not believe in God.

Third, there are those who believe that there is no God; i.e. the non-existence of God is established by conclusive arguments. All the same, they really base their belief not on such arguments, but on the assertion that there is no evidence for the existence of God. However, they present some arguments only incidentally. These people form a small minority, and probably account for less than one percent of all atheists.

The stand of the three groups can be summarised as 'rejection due to lack of proof', 'rejection and denial due to the lack of possibility of proof or disproof', and 'rejection due to proof of non-existence', in this order. The first group is the largest in number, the third are very few in number, and the second are a little more than [the third]. The atheists in Europe and America have chosen for themselves the name 'agnostics', which literally means that they just do not know. They have taken the stand that they have no evidence of the existence of God; not that they have proof of His non-existence. Thus, a large majority of atheists do not believe in God because they have no evidence of His existence. Here it is not our purpose to refute the beliefs of these people, because the refutation of this stand covers this presentation so far, supplementing each positive argument by dismissing various doubts. Other positive arguments relating to the next section will, God willing, be stated as and when appropriate. The same applies to the refutation of views of the second category. Here, I intend to refute the ideas of the third group who claim that non-existence of God is established by arguments. I will only state facts which have not been mentioned above, avoiding any unnecessary repetition. Such atheists put forward the following arguments in support of their belief.

The First Argument for Atheism and Its Refutation

The first argument presented by atheists in support of their belief is based on the fact that there can be only two possibilities about the creation of this universe. Either it has been created by a Higher Being, or it has existed by itself since eternity or a particular time and runs by itself in accordance with some inherent mechanism and system of cause and effect. There is no other possibility. Both these scenarios are beyond human comprehension, since we cannot understand how something, God or the universe, can exist by itself since eternity or since a particular time. However, if we have to accept one of the two scenarios, it is by far easier, simpler, and safer to accept that this universe rather than a Higher Being is self-existent.

A detailed refutation of this view has been given in the section dealing with the argument for the existence of God on the basis of this universe, and need not be repeated here. It was established there in full detail that this whole enterprise that we call the universe and the Being of God—the Exalted, the Maker of the universe—are two different things by virtue of their attributes, properties, and conditions and can therefore not be treated on an equal footing. Neither can it be understood that accepting both as 'having been in existence on its own since eternity' carries the same meaning [for each]. The truth is that, whereas God, on account of His attributes of Godhead, demands that He be accepted as Eternal and Supreme, having no being above Him, the state of the universe and all that it contains prove that they have not existed on their own since eternity. There is nothing to rule out that there exists a Higher Being above them. The difference is obvious. The two can certainly not be treated alike. The idea that it is easier, simpler, and safer to accept that this world has existed forever is completely erroneous and creates many insoluble problems. On the contrary, it is easier to understand, simpler, and safer to accept that this universe is created and its Creator is Eternal. Moreover, there are other arguments for the existence of God, as discussed earlier. If necessary, the reader can revisit the earlier discussion concerning this matter. It is not necessary to repeat it here.

The Second Argument for Atheism and Its Refutation

The second argument presented by atheists in support of their belief is that the laws of nature and the law of cause and effect operating in the universe are so perfect and elaborate that there is absolutely no need for a Creator or a Higher Being. The unnecessary belief in God is mere superstition. This argument has also been refuted above and it was explained why, despite a perfect law, a Higher Being is still required. It was also clarified that, the law of cause and effect notwithstanding, presence of design in this universe and purpose of life argues for a Creator and a Controller. The reader may refer to the appropriate section, if necessary. It has not been realised that the law of cause and effect itself requires a Maker and a Supervisor. The causes and effects are like tools a craftsman uses to prepare things, and the end products prove the existence of the craftsman. Thus, the law of cause and effect cannot be used as an argument against the existence of God. On the contrary, the law and its effect in giving particular direction and design to the universe constitute an undeniable proof for existence of a Higher Being, which no intelligent person can deny.

The Third Argument for Atheism and Its Refutation

The third argument presented by atheists is based on the theory of evolution which, they claim, shows that everything in our world has not always been as it is. Instead, initially it was in a primitive state and gradually evolved to its present state, adapting to environments with the passage of time. The species that failed to adapt to their environments became extinct. From this, they conclude that there is no inherent plan or design in this universe and that it all happened by chance.

We have already refuted this argument in principle. It should be kept in mind that the extinction of some species because of their failure to adapt to the environment and gradual adaptation of the others does not prove that the world is without a plan or design. On the contrary, extinction of some species and survival of the others denotes an underlying wisdom and proves that there is a design and final cause for this universe and purpose of life. It indicates that the Creator of this universe is constantly pruning His garden and trimming the trees therein. He cuts down the branches and plants that are weak to allow for the progress of a stronger tree and removes weaker trees so they do not hinder the progress of the stronger ones.

One might argue that if God knew that a particular branch or tree of this garden of the universe is weak and unable to fulfil the purpose of its creation, why did He create it in the first place? God did indeed create everything with a particular purpose to fulfil. However, when it develops a defect and cannot keep pace with others and fails to fulfil the purpose of its creation, it is dropped in accordance with the law of nature. Both laws are made by God. One, that God creates everything with a specific purpose and He wants it to fulfil the purpose. Second, when something is adversely affected and fails to fulfil its purpose, it is destroyed. For instance, God created man for spiritual and physical progress but because of their misdeeds, some do not fulfil the purpose and are thereby cut off like dry branches.

It should also be born in mind that according to the law of nature, the sole purpose of some species is to support others in their growth for a limited period. Once the latter are firmly established and have attained their perfection, the supporting species are rendered extinct. Farmers sometimes grow 'fillers' around some plants to protect them and enhance their growth. Once the plants become strong, the fillers are destroyed for they have fulfilled their purpose and their preservation thereafter may prove harmful for the plants.

Science further shows that the death of certain organisms provides life and sustenance for the others. The sole purpose of their creation is to die and give birth to life and growth of others. There are countless other examples to demonstrate that the extinction of some species after a time, and survival and growth of the others, does not disprove the existence of God. What it does prove is that there is a Conscious, Wise and Omniscient Being who has the capacity and wisdom to run this universe toward a particular goal.

Someone may yet ask: If the weak are destroyed and only the strong survive in accordance with the law of nature, then where is the Hand of God? I maintain that we do not deny the laws of nature and we do believe in this law of cause and effect, but these do not disprove the existence of God. As already elaborated, the system of cause and effect itself points to a Higher Being and constitutes another evidence for the existence of God. I would like to reiterate that the theory of evolution as postulated by Darwin is not an established scientific fact. Some of its details have been disputed by many other scientists and the theory in its present form has been totally rejected.

The Fourth Argument for Atheism and Its Refutation

The fourth argument presented by atheists against the existence of God is also based on the theory of evolution. It is claimed that the religious teachings about the creation of the universe and creation of the human beings is shown to be inaccurate in light of the theory of evolution. This proves that the religious teachings are false and contrary to evidence, thus disproving the concept of God as presented by the religious teachings. This question has also been addressed in detail.

The Fifth Argument for Atheism and Its Refutation

The fifth argument presented by atheists is that the law of nature attributed to a Higher Being is random and sometimes acts ruthlessly. The randomness of this law is proof in itself that this cannot be the work of a wise being. On the contrary, they argue that by studying the laws of nature, it becomes clear that the universe runs on natural transformation and the system of cause and effect. They give the examples of disasters afflicting innocent people leading to loss of life and suffering, epidemics of diseases, birth of physically and mentally disabled children, and personal decline after a period of success. They say that these occurrences of daily life prove that there is no God, otherwise such indiscriminate calamities and misfortunes would never take place. This objection has not been dealt with so far and needs to be answered in some detail.

It is Essential to Distinguish
the Law of Nature from the Law of Shariah

The objection has arisen because the critics have not reflected deeply on two sets of laws enforced in this world by God. They think that the whole world is functioning under one set of laws. The truth is that God has ordained two different sets of laws for this world. One is the law of nature which relates to the organisation of this universe. This comprises of the system of cause and effect and the properties of various elements. We observe the impact of this law at all times. The second is the law of Shariah, which relates to the moral and spiritual aspects of man and is revealed through Prophets and Messengers, and it operates on the principle of reward and punishment that will be experienced in the life after death. The above objection has arisen as a result of mixing up the two sets of laws and not properly differentiating between them.

What is the law of nature? The law of nature is that everything, every motion and every stillness, as well as each and every object of the world, has an innate ability to exert a certain effect. For example, the law of nature is that, if ingested in a certain quantity, arsenic will kill a living being, unless another law of nature counteracts the actions of arsenic and nullifies its effect. Likewise, it is in keeping with the law of nature that when a critical point of weakness has been reached, the roof will collapse and would kill anyone who is underneath unless another law of nature intervenes to save this person. Similarly, it is in keeping with the law of nature that a person who does not know how to swim will drown in deep waters unless an alternative way of nature saves him through an intervention. Thus, it is part of nature that anything, no matter how advanced, will be adversely affected if it does not have the ability to counter the power of harmful and damaging forces. All this, and countless others, are part of the law of nature whereby everything produces its natural effect and the wheels of this great machine are perpetually set in motion. These laws do not discriminate between friend or foe. Under normal circumstances, in pursuance of the duties assigned to them, they are obliged to raise up or drop down, push forward or pull backwards anyone who is at the receiving end. (There are exceptions, which pertain to special Divine decrees under a special independent law and are manifested in the form of miracles and acceptance of prayers through the Prophets and *Auliyā*.)

As opposed to the above: What is the law of Shariah? It is the law and the code of conduct revealed by God for the followers of a religion so that they reform their morals, get closer to God, and partake of the favours and the blessings reserved for the righteous. Under this law, everyone is granted the free will to abide by it or not, and the reward or retribution of one's deeds is determined in the life after death (except for some veiled effects that appear in this world). For instance, Shariah urges people to worship God in a prescribed way in order to attain His nearness and pleasure, but does not force them to do so. If one wants to defy it, he is free to do so and is not forced to follow this law. The effects of this defiance may appear in this world in a subtle way, but the real and definite punishment is deferred to the hereafter. There is a saying among the sages: this world is the place for deeds and the next is the place for reward and punishment.

As for the law of nature, however, this world is both for deeds and for recompense. The two laws do not interfere with each other except in exceptional circumstances, the mention of which here is not necessary. Anyone who violates the law of nature is not spared the consequences on the grounds that he did not violate the law of the Shariah. He will certainly suffer the consequences of violating the law of nature, and compliance with the law of Shariah cannot save him from that. Consider, for example, if a roof collapsed on two people, one pious and the other a sinner: in accordance with the law of nature, both will die or both will survive, depending on the way the roof fell. It would not [simply] be the case that the pious one is saved and the evil one dies. Similarly, if a pious and God-fearing person, who does not know how to swim, jumps into deep water, he will not be saved from drowning merely because he is pious. His piety relates to the law of Shariah and water is under the law of nature. The law of nature normally is not influenced by the law of Shariah.

In short, as a general rule, the law of Shariah only determines the recompense of a good or bad deed within Shariah and has no bearing on the recompense determined by the law of nature, and vice versa. It is absurd for the atheists to support their belief with this. As for instance, a pious and righteous person who had young children went for a bath in the river and drowned whereas an evil person bathing in the river at the same time returned home safe and sound; a very chaste and well behaved girl caught fire and died a day after her marriage while an unchaste and ill-mannered girl married the same day lived happily ever after; an innocent and good-natured boy was crushed to death by a falling roof whereas an evil and filthy boy playing there went out moments earlier and escaped harm etc. On the basis of such instances, the atheists argue that if there was a God such outrage and injustice would not have taken place.

If one thinks carefully, this objection is weak and absurd. The person who drowned violated the law of nature and suffered accordingly, though he conformed to the Shariah; the other had not violated the law of nature and, therefore, was not liable to any penalty under that law though he was on the wrong side of the law of Shariah. The same applies to the girl who caught fire and died—she fell afoul of the law of nature and perished. That was determined by the law of nature, and conforming to the Shariah was of no avail. The other girl, though guilty of contravention of Shariah, escaped any punishment under the law of nature as she did not violate any law of nature.

So there is no disorder or injustice. The laws of nature treat everyone as an equal. Indeed, it would be most unfair if the laws of nature punished people even if they have broken no law or if people were punished through the laws of nature for breaking the laws of Shariah or vice versa. This is not how it all works; nature punishes for violation of its laws and Shariah punishes for violation of its laws (with exceptions that form another topic altogether and need not be mentioned here). This cannot be regarded as objectionable or unwise by any sane person.

I wonder what kind of wisdom and intelligence critics have to raise such objections; how can they consider a process full of wisdom which breaks no law, and does not create any conflict between the two sets of laws, as contrary to justice. Unfortunately, all this is a result of a big misunderstanding, when the reason for an incident which takes place under the law of nature is sought in the law of Shariah—and when they fail to find an explanation, they call it unfair. O ye unfortunate one! May God bestow wisdom upon you. Seek explanation of natural occurrences in the law of nature, and of Shariah punishment in the law of Shariah. Then you will come to realise that there is no injustice at all; in fact, what you are suggesting is injustice. Indeed, it is a great injustice to suggest that an accidental death of a person by burning, drowning, or a collapsed building, which is in concordance with the laws of nature, cannot be fair because he has committed no sin according to the law of Shariah. Most regrettably, it is preposterous to attribute the law of Shariah for acts of nature and vice versa and then blame God for this!

Remember, Shariah and nature are two separate laws that do not interfere with the affairs of each other just like civilised worldly governments. However, under very special circumstances, God may command one set of laws to come into action in order to support the other. For instance, when Prophets and Messengers are ordained and there is eagerness in the heavens for reformation of the world, the forces of nature are made subservient to the cause of Shariah. Such exceptional decrees are manifested as miracles and Divine signs. In general, however, the law of nature and law of Shariah act independently of each other and neither interfere with, nor step aside for, each other. The whole misconception stems from amalgamating the two sets of laws and failing to recognise them as independent entities.

Transmigration of Souls

The doctrine of transmigration of souls, or reincarnation, is also based on a similar misunderstanding. Those who believe in this doctrine argue that children are born in different situations as a result of their actions in a past life. That is why some babies are born weak or healthy, blind or sighted, able-bodied or disabled, intelligent or unintelligent, and rich or poor. Otherwise, they ask—if there was no previous life and no record of good and bad deeds—how do we explain the difference? Could we say that God is unjust in bringing children of the same species into the world under such diverse circumstances? If not, then there is no explanation other than a previous life.

The believers in reincarnation have also failed to see the difference between the law of Shariah and law of nature, and use one law to measure everything. They have not realised that differences at birth are not related to the law of Shariah, but have to do with the law of nature. The child inherits the physical, economical and moral conditions of his parents and ancestors, which vary from family to family.

Medical science, which is based on the law of nature, has established that if parents are healthy, the children are likely to be healthy but if the parents are fragile, so shall be the children. Even physical features are inherited by children. This science is so vast and established by repeated experiments and observations that it cannot be refuted. It has also been shown that the condition of man and woman at the time of conception of a baby also deeply affects the child. In view of this, the Islamic Shariah has very wisely advised men and women to purify their hearts and minds when they try for a baby so that the child should inherit their purity of mind. In short, medical science has found that effects of the parents and ancestors are passed down to the children, and it is because of this that some children are born healthy while others are weak. Some are born normal while others have some birth defects.

There is a general law of nature, also mentioned in the Holy Quran, that everything has an impact on its surroundings (16:49). Everything in this world depends on others for its survival and everything can be influenced by other things in the universe. Thus, an offspring, which is the closest to his parents, is influenced by the good and bad traits of his parents. So the notion that babies are born with different characteristics as a result of their deeds in a previous birth is erroneous and absurd. This misunderstanding arises because people seek the cause of acts of nature in the law of Shariah.

The ideas of atheists and those who believe in reincarnation are based on the same error. Both have failed to identify the distinction between the law of nature and law of Shariah; they have sought the cause of acts of nature in the law of Shariah. As they were unable to find a reasonable explanation, one group concluded that it was all anarchy and the idea of God was baseless. The others argued that God is not unjust and would not punish anyone without reason. So, the disparity among newborn children must be rooted in their previous births, hence the doctrine of reincarnation. Had they pondered, they would have easily understood that God has ordained two sets of laws acting independently of each other and it is a grave error to seek the cause of acts of nature in the laws of Shariah.

To summarise, the righteous and the innocent sometimes suffer during natural calamities, diseases, and disasters. This is only because the law of nature is different from the law of Shariah. A good deed in conformity with Shariah, on its own, cannot protect one from the penalties incurred under the law of nature. For this, precautions prescribed in the law of nature are required. For instance, the event of drowning follows the laws of nature and a righteous person will have to learn to swim and take other precautions to save himself from drowning, just like anyone else. Just being righteous will not save him from drowning in water. Similarly, the birth of a disabled baby is an act of nature and seeking its cause in the Shariah is pointless. Here, parents need to turn to the law of nature and parents should seek the cure for their sickness, weakness, and defects, and focus on improving the environmental factors that lead to such disabilities.

It is Essential for Human Progress that the Law of Nature Remains Separate and Independent of the Shariah

One may ask why the law of nature does not submit to the law of the Shariah and why a righteous and God-fearing person is not saved from mishaps and misfortunes. The first answer, as already explained, is that the two laws are different and work independently, yet the scenario presented by the objector requires that the two laws amalgamate. However, their separate existence indicates that they were meant to remain independent.

The second and actual answer is that God ordained the two sets of laws for two kinds of progress of man: the law of nature leads to material progress and the law of Shariah is required for moral and spiritual progress. If conformity with the law of Shariah were to protect against the ill consequences of the violation of the law of nature, this would have hindered one's material progress. For instance, if the righteousness of a man were to protect him from drowning, burning, or electrical hazards, then he would have no motivation to learn about or understand harmful processes, or to find ways to control them.

Remember, the material progress of a person is possible only because he knows that unless he studies the laws of nature and properties of matter, he will not be able to discover the means of welfare, comfort, and progress for himself. That is why man is always engaged in the study of nature and properties of elements. They say, 'necessity is the mother of invention'. If the material needs of man are fulfilled merely by conforming to Shariah, then nobody will waste their time in the study of nature and properties of elements. All material progress will come to a standstill and material knowledge will come to an end. Therefore, it is pure Divine grace that the two laws (of nature and Shariah) do not interfere with each other. Some calamities are also fore-runners of this blessing, as after facing calamities, one develops awareness and motivation to find ways to avoid these in the future. Thus, measures taken after the loss of a few lives lead to saving millions of lives from future hazards.

In short, both of these laws are meant to bring about different kinds of progress for mankind. If the two laws were to amalgamate or give way to each other, it would be very harmful and detrimental for the progress of mankind. The fact is that the parallel working of these two laws is entirely appropriate and highly judicious for the collective welfare and progress of mankind, and one cannot think of anything better.

Sometimes, pious and righteous people meet apparently

untimely deaths as a result of accidents or some other law of nature, leaving their relatives in a state of extraordinary shock or loss. According to the teaching of Islam, God provides for the bereaved family out of His mercy in some other ways. God enforces His law for the welfare and progress of the world and does not break His law for anyone under normal circumstances. However, He is, at the same time, very kind to His good people and most faithful to them. Therefore, on such occasions, He most surely compensates their losses by some other means. For example, for sufferings in this world, He grants them special reward in the Hereafter, generously provides for their progeny the blessings of this world, or demonstrates some other means of Mercy and Justice without compromising the rights of others.

As for the children who are born with weakness and disability which hinder their spiritual progress, Islam teaches us that God will consider their disability on the Day of Judgement. They will not be accountable for deeds which were beyond their control nor will they suffer any loss of reward because of their physical debility. God says in the Quran that His law of recompense takes into account every act of goodness for reward and does not ignore any extenuating factor.

Why is there Sin in the World?

It is essential to dispel another doubt here. Why is there sin, injustice, and transgression in the world? It is argued that if God existed, people would never freely indulge in sin, injustice, and tyranny and the world would be free of evil. These critics have not understood the purpose and philosophy of the law of Shariah. Shariah provides people with a code of conduct and explains that they need to adhere to it, and their moral and spiritual progress cannot take place without this. After this explanation, people are given the choice to accept or reject this code of conduct. The one who accepts this code of conduct is rewarded with blessings and piety according to his level of commitment, and gains nearness to God. One who chooses to reject this code of conduct deprives himself from its blessings. This rejection of Divine code of conduct is also called sin and transgression. Therefore, sin is not created by God, but is [the result of] the deeds of man. Therefore, to argue against God, because there is sin in this world or infer that sin happens because there is no God, is erroneous and absolutely absurd.

God has sown the seed of good in human nature, and to prosper and flourish this seed, He has revealed His Shariah. Then, through His signs and revelations, [He has] made it crystal clear that their prosperity and salvation lies in adhering to the code of conduct of the Shariah. Despite this, if someone chooses not to follow God's Shariah, then it is the fault of that person and not of God. He is deprived as a result of his own doing and not an act of God. What is sin? It is an act of disobedience of God and to follow a path against the guidance of God. Thus, sin results from one's own conduct. Should God have refrained from guiding us only because some people would not follow His guidance? Do you expect a father to stop advising his son for fear that the son may become guilty of disobeying him? These are arguments of ignorance and every wise person should avoid them.

To summarise, the sins and injustices are brought about by

peoples' own doings and God bears no responsibility for this. No sensible person can argue against the existence of God on account of sin. What God has ordained is sheer and absolute mercy. The one who fails to benefit from this mercy is accountable for his own deeds.

One may ask: why did God not frame the Shariah law such that it was not possible to break it and everyone would be compelled to adhere to this? In this case, they maintain, there would be no sin and everyone would be pious and virtuous. The answer to this question is that under such circumstances, the very purpose of man's creation would have been lost. The purpose is that man should make progress through his own efforts and, through his righteous deeds, qualify to become a recipient of God's favours and honours—ultimately, gaining His nearness. If everyone was forced to conform to the Divinely revealed Shariah, all the doors of progress would be closed on man. No one would merit favours and honours, and all effort and struggle would be in vain. It has to be understood that, to merit favours, man must be free to choose between good and evil of his own free will. If man was under compulsion to adopt a certain path, then there would be no distinction between those who love righteousness and those who do not; those who follow the right path and those who do not; those who exercise self-control and those who do not; those who hold steadfast and those who do not; those who work hard and those who do not. No difference would exist between a doer of good and an evil-doer. Likewise, the progress that can be achieved, through competition to excel one another in acts of goodness, would come to a standstill. There would be no motivation to make progress. Man would freeze in a static condition, or become like an angel who is compelled by his creation to stick to the right path and cannot, even slightly, deviate from God's Will. The wise say that the righteous man has a rank above angels because man adopts virtue of his preference after due consideration, whereas an angel is confined in a state of virtue and therefore the good deeds of an angel are not counted as such. That is why the Quran says about man:

$$\text{لَقَدْ خَلَقْنَا الْإِنْسَانَ فِيٓ اَحْسَنِ تَقْوِيمٍ}^{1}$$

Surely, of all the creation, *We have created man in the best make.* No other creation compares with man.

In short, man's free will is a mark of his excellence and sin results from misuse of this will. Sin is not created by God, but results from denial of God's Mercy. Sin, therefore, cannot be presented as an argument against the existence of God.

Sixth Argument for Atheism and Its Refutation

The sixth argument, like the fifth, is also based on an assumed injustice attributed to the laws of nature. The atheists say that there are many things in the world that do not serve any useful purpose and are obviously harmful. For instance, there are countless harmful animals and poisonous shrubs and creepers and deadly minerals that are only harmful and have no benefits at all.

---

1. *Sūrah at-Tīn,* 95:5.

That, according to them, proves that there is no God. Otherwise, such things would not exist. It demonstrates their ignorance. In fact, there is nothing in this world that is useless and does not serve any purpose. It is due only to a lack of knowledge that man does not understand the purpose of certain things, is ignorant of their benefits, and forms his opinion after seeing some of their harmful effects. It is rare for those who are well-versed with the reality of things to raise such objections. The laymen fall victim to such doubts only because they have little knowledge about the reality of things, and they do not look beyond the superficial forms and functions of things, and are not accustomed to deep and profound study. Those with more extensive study, who are used to getting to the bottom of realities, fully understand that everything has some benefit in it and the more a thing is studied, the more obvious its purpose and benefits becomes. If such people do not find any benefit in something until an appointed time, they do not regard it as useless. Rather, they continue to believe that a deeper study in the future will unearth some benefits in it. They have learnt from repeated experiences that many benefits are discovered in apparently useless and harmful things after deep study and research. The fact is that everything in this world has some benefit in it. As man advances in the study of the reality of things, his belief that nothing in this world is useless becomes stronger and more certain.

Critics do not realise that in the past, when knowledge about the reality of things was limited and people were far less inclined towards science, more things appeared useless and harmful as compared to today. The study of the reality of things and scientific research has discovered benefits in many of those things and explained their harmful effects, too. It can even be proved that this harmfulness is indirectly beneficial for mankind. That should make one think that many of the things appearing useless and harmful today will appear full of hidden benefits tomorrow and, still later, the knowledge and insight about them will expand further. The knowledge will go on increasing as a result of new sciences and research and ignorance will go on decreasing. It is written in the Holy Quran and *aḥādīth* that in the latter days the hidden treasures of the heaven and the earth will be disclosed and new sciences will flourish. Thus, it would be the height of ignorance to deny the benefits of countless things and, on account of some of their harmful effects, or on the basis of the current state of knowledge, believe them to be harmful. As explained above, even these harmful effects are based on the subtle wisdom of nature and mankind and other creatures indirectly benefit from them in many ways.

But for the fear of prolonging this book, I could have listed many animals, plants, and minerals which were considered useless and harmful in the past but are today serving mankind. Even snakes, scorpions, organisms causing fatal diseases, and poisons of various types, etc., are not excluded from service to mankind. No new day dawns when the saying of the Holy Quran that God has not created anything in the heaven and the earth in vain[1] is not vindicated.

---

1. *Sūrah Ṣād,* 38:28.

Why are there Harmful Things in the World?

It may well be asked that if God has not created anything without purpose, and everything has been made for the benefit of man, why do some things cause harm, and why were these things not created beneficial without having any harmful aspects? For example, the benefit man and other creatures derive from snakes should have been provided without any harmful side effects. The first answer is that the Creator did what He considered appropriate. We have neither the right nor the ability to criticise the acts of nature. Our job is to find out whether or not whatever is happening in the world is primarily and collectively based on truth, justice, and mercy. When it has been proved that nothing in this world is entirely harmful but has definite benefits hidden in it, and even the things that appear useless and harmful are not really so but appear so because of the lack of our knowledge, then it is most inappropriate to find faults with nature and to ask why something is this way or that way. No wise person can expect that man, who is himself one of the creation, could have such deep insight into the principles of creation that he should be able to tell with certainty the principles underlying the creation of each and everything. So that is my first answer: when something has been established in principle, then it is inappropriate to go on raising random questions, one after another.

Moreover, if we only accept things after all their intricacies have been resolved, then no debate will ever come to an end as such questions would continue to be raised indefinitely. It is only logical that when a thing has been understood in principle, even though some details have yet to be resolved, we should accept it and leave the rest to God.

Now I come to the actual answer. Harmfulness of certain things is expedient in that they sometimes help produce beneficial results. For example, snake venom is used as a remedy in some deadly diseases and, under the law of nature, this beneficial effect is inseparably linked with its poisonous effect. This harmfulness is also beneficial and advantageous in that it helps to indirectly promote moral reformation and material progress. Every wise person will agree with me that occasional hardships and misfortunes are essential for the perfection of man's morals. One who has never faced hardships and misfortunes in his life cannot achieve perfection of his morals. Similarly, material progress is not possible without such challenges. Therefore, harmfulness in certain things is indirectly conducive to man's benefit and progress. There must be many more, as yet undiscovered, benefits in it.

One may ask, if these dangerous animals are actually beneficial for man, why are they destroyed and why does religion itself sometimes order us to keep killing them? As a general rule, nature requires a balance in everything, avoiding any gross deviation from the norm. The excess of things with obvious deleterious effects can cause more harm than good. Such things can remain predominantly beneficial if their number does not exceed a certain limit. Therefore, in His ultimate wisdom, God has created these things and at the same time invested man with the tendency, and in certain cases explicitly ordered man, to prevent their excess beyond a certain limit. In this way, the balance of nature has been established.

To summarise, that some things in this world have some

harmful aspects is not an objectionable fact. The fact remains that everything in the world is created with a purpose and harmfulness of some things is also indirectly beneficial for man. Therefore, this objection by the atheists is absurd and baseless and only proves their ignorance.

The Seventh Argument for Atheism and Its Refutation: Freud's Theory

The seventh argument presented by some atheists is based on the theories of some European philosophers that the concept of God is no more than a product of the human mind. They believe that whereas a child has a powerful bond of love with his father, is naturally inclined towards him, admires him, and feels protected by him, a child also fears his father and considers him to be a danger. But the child does not harbour such feelings about his mother, as he gets food directly from her. Its sentiments of love for his mother are greater and warmer and prevail over all other sentiments. The child never regards its mother as a source of fear or danger and runs to her under all circumstances. Therefore, an ingenious and ambitious son may develop sentiments of jealousy and rivalry subconsciously towards his father, but never against his mother. Western philosophers have termed it 'the Oedipus complex' on the basis of an old Greek story about a young man who killed his father inadvertently and then married his mother unknowingly. These philosophers believe that a child develops a kind of jealousy and fear for his father and at the same time has innate love for him and regards him as a means of protection. Consequently, as he grows up and out of his father's shadow, he feels a vacuum in his mind in which the 'father-son' image is firmly established. This vacuum leads him to an imaginary being to replace his father figure and that imaginary being ultimately develops into a god.

This theory is largely presented by a renowned European philosopher and scientist, Sigmund Freud, who was born to a Jewish family in Austria in 1856 and later migrated to England and died in 1954. He wrote many books and is considered an authority on human psychology. From this viewpoint, he raised many objections about the concept of God and the philosophy of dreams. On the topic under discussion, he writes:

> In this way the mother, who satisfies the child's hunger, becomes its first object of love and certainly also its first protection against all the undefined dangers which threaten it in the external world; its first protection against anxiety, we may say. In this function [of protection] the mother is soon replaced by the stronger father, who retains that position for the rest of childhood. But the child's attitude toward its father is coloured by a particular ambivalence. The father himself constitutes a danger for the child, perhaps because of his [father's] earlier relation to its mother. Thus it fears him no less than it longs for him and admires him. [...] When the growing individual finds that he is destined to remain a child forever, that he can never do without protection against strange superior powers, he lends those powers the features belonging to the figure of father. He creates himself the gods whom he dreads, whom he seeks to propitiate, and whom he nevertheless entrusts

with his protection. Thus, his longing for a father figure is a motive identical with his need for protection against consequences of his human weakness. The defence against childish helplessness is what lends its characteristic features to the adult's reaction to the helplessness which he has to acknowledge—a reaction which is precisely the formation of religion. (*The Future of an Illusion,* pp. 41–42, Sigmund Freud)

Freud has further elaborated his theory in his writings and has also written a great deal about the Oedipus Complex. Though many Western philosophers have rejected Freud's theory, it is necessary that we analyse it briefly.

First of all, it should be realised that this theory is an offshoot of another theory which we have discussed in the beginning in the context of 'universal acceptance' and is based on what is generally known as, 'Inferiority Complex'; i.e. a feeling of weakness and inferiority before a superior and more powerful being. We have already sufficiently dealt with this in the aforementioned discussion and need not repeat it. However, it is particularly remarkable in that although a Jew himself, whether he was aware of it or not, Freud seems to have borrowed this idea from Christianity as he spent his life in Christian surroundings. Jesus, in contrast to the dry and philosophical religious teachings of Judaism, presented God metaphorically as a father figure. The Christians later on started believing in God as Father and Jesus as the real son of God. This 'father-son' concept is well-known and publicised amongst Christians everywhere. In spite of being a Jew, a competent scientist, and an authority on human psychology, Freud's mind could not resist the effect of his surroundings. As he was not a Christian, it would not be surprising if he might have thought that Jesus, too, suffered from an inferiority complex! *O sagacity, you have become a calamity for me!*

The problem is that sometimes even sensible people do not distinguish between the possibility of something happening and that which has actually happened. During their intellectual pursuits, they look for the grounds for a possibility, and when they are convinced that something could have happened in a particular way, they blindly jump to the conclusion that it must have happened that way. Obviously, possibility is one thing and something actually happening is quite another. There are millions of things that can happen in this world, but how many of them actually happen? It is naïve to argue that something has happened just because it can. Let us assume that jealousy can develop subconsciously in a son at times; and that, consequently, he feels a vacuum in his mind when he grows up as he keeps looking for his childhood father-figure; and that this mental vacuum sometimes leads him to the idea of a Higher Being to replace this father-figure. In spite of all these remote possibilities, how can it be proved that all these things actually happened this way amongst all the nations, who were at least initially isolated from each other, in different parts of the world, at different times?

Strangely enough, even if we accept that all these possibilities are valid, they are vague and far-fetched compared to other possibilities. For instance, even if it is correct that the son can develop jealousy towards his father under certain circumstances, it is obvious, as our experience shows, that it happens very rarely. By and large, the son remains loving and faithful to his father. Even if he excels his father, he remains humble to his father with innate love and devotion. Thus, the assumed possibility is far-fetched and the same applies to other possibilities understood by the Western philosophers. Thus, generally speaking, the theory of jealousy and a mental vacuum is no more than mere conjecture. To adopt an unnatural walkway in preference to a natural highway and deny God, who has been accepted by every nation throughout the ages, on the basis of a far-fetched possibility, is no more than wishful thinking. Evidently, those who present such arguments have first denied the existence of God and then devised these arguments.

The inferiority complex presented by some scholars as an argument against the existence of God is, in fact, a weighty argument for the existence of God. Muslim scholars have always presented it as such. Ḥaḍrat Aliᵗᵃ, the fourth Caliph of the Holy Prophetˢᵃʷ, said:

$$\text{عَرَفْتُ رَبِّیْ بِفَسْخِ الْعَزَائِمِ}$$

Meaning that, I have recognised God by the failure of many a firm resolve and sound plans.

This brief statement of Ḥaḍrat Aliᵗᵃ is full of profound insight and incorporates the philosophy otherwise referred to as 'inferiority complex' and used by those who are unaware of spirituality to argue against the existence of God. Ḥaḍrat Aliᵗᵃ means to say that man sometimes makes a firm resolve, devises a solid plan, and acquires all the necessary means to achieve something and thinks that he is almost there. Then suddenly, out of the blue, something happens that unravels all his plans and shatters his resolve. It is then that man realises that his resolve and his plans are not the whole thing but there is a Being higher than man's plans and stronger than his resolve. Compared to Him, man, with all his intelligence and wisdom and all the material sources, amounts to nothing. It is this realisation of inferiority that always leads the wise to God, but, regrettably, Western scholars have chosen the same concept to stumble upon.

The core of the theory put forward by Freud and the like-minded scholars is that man has innate quest for a Higher and more Powerful Being, to be a model for him, whose superior knowledge and power should be awe-inspiring and whom he might take as his protector. This central point of their theory argues in favour of existence of God, not against it. As stated in the beginning of this book, the Holy Quran has presented it as evidence of *fitrah* supporting the existence of God. Thus the claim that as the child grows up the father-figure leaves a vacuum, which is then filled by an imaginary god is absurd and contrary to human nature and our observation. It is true, of course, that without belief in God, human nature does experience a vacuum which ultimately attracts fortunate ones to God. Hence, from whichever angle we look at it, this argument presented by Freud and other like-minded people is no more than a philosophical conjecture. The fact is that this argument is in favour of God's existence rather than against it, and that is why many other Western scholars have rejected it.

These were the seven basic arguments presented by atheists to support their doctrine. However, all these arguments originate not from one but several schools of thought and, therefore, some of them contradict each other. I have put all such arguments together as I intended to refute all of them. I hope that after understanding the refutation of these seven basic arguments, every learned person would be able to respond to atheists. The atheists really have no arguments and the basis of their denial is that they think they have not come across any strong evidence of the existence of God to convince and satisfy them. The more prudent among them do not positively rule out the existence of God for that shifts the onus, the burden they cannot cope with. They take the stand that they have no evidence for the existence of God. Those who have gone through my book carefully, with good intentions, must have realised that logical arguments for the existence of God are so strong that no wise person can continue, at the very least, to deny God after understanding them. As I stated in the beginning, the logical arguments can only provide us with elementary level of certainty about the existence of God, but not the utmost certainty. For the latter, we need different types of arguments which pertain to experience and observation; we come to know them through miracles and signs of the Prophets and the Righteous.

Communism and God

Some people regard communism as a branch of atheism and one of the proofs of the non-existence of God. In fact, communism is merely an economic system which has nothing to do with the existence or non-existence of God. Just as some impulsive people declared that evolution is evidence against the existence of God, others have come to think that communism does the same. Communism, whether it is right or wrong, has nothing to do with the issue of the existence of God. It is merely an economic system whereby Russia took over the control of resources in an effort to justly distribute the country's wealth, so they believe. They have stumbled in this effort and the harmful effects are being felt insidiously even now as evidenced by perpetual changes in the system but more obvious effects will surface after a few generations. In any case, communism is merely an economic system and has nothing to do with existence of God. Nevertheless, it made its headway by disrupting other systems including those attributed to religions. Thus, apparently, a confrontation has developed between this system and the teachings of religions.

The second reason for this confrontation was that the communist leaders abolished religious teaching in the schools to indoctrinate the youth with communism, and to exclude the impact of any anti-communist ideas. That has led to the spread of atheism in the country, but atheism is not part of communism. Instead, it is a consequence of factors surrounding it. There is nothing in communism itself which could be taken as an argument against the existence of God. The principles and some details of the communist system are, undoubtedly, against the teachings of known religions and contain, from a purely academic point of view, several dangerous elements that will unfold their formidable effects after a few generations. In any case, fundamentally, communism is an economic system—not religious or spiritual. So it is not right to present it in support of atheism.

For centuries, the European economic system had resulted in the accumulation of wealth of nations in the hands of a few capitalists, while the rest of the population struggled in dire straits of poverty. The situation deteriorated to such an extent that desperate measures to change the system were inevitable. The situation was most dreadful in Russia where the tyrannical rule of the Tsars and extravagant living of the rich had strangled the poor. Long periods of injustice always evoke a reaction that takes the form of rebellion against the established system. A similar reaction took place in Russia in the form of communism which laid the foundation of a new system through a brutal revolution. The reign of the Tsars ended, barons lost their ranks, the rich lost their riches, and the communist system was introduced for apparently equal sharing of the country's wealth. Like every reaction and rebellion against an established system, communism turned from one extreme to the other. Obviously, both the extremes are equally dangerous, though these dangers may not be apparent immediately. Very briefly, the dangers are:

1. By taking over all the wealth and resources of the country, the state deprived the individual of the greatest incentive for hard work and industry. There are many incentives for work, but the most common one, that is found equally among all people of all classes and is part of human nature, is the desire to benefit from the fruit of one's own labour. This desire and eagerness was crushed totally by communism. Indeed, every decent person has a desire to lend a hand to others and to spend a part of his wealth for their needs and Islam has emphasised that a great deal. The great natural incentive, however, is to know that man will enjoy the greater part of the fruit of his own labour. Communism has destroyed this incentive and slowed down human progress.

2. The second big drawback of communism is that, with all the resources in the hands of the government, the spirit to compete and excel each other will start waning, inevitably resulting in gradual national decline. For instance, when several individuals or firms, in addition to the state, are engaged in the manufacturing of cars or aircraft, and trying to promote the industry through hard work and research and with healthy rivalry and competition, the industry will flourish a great deal. By contrast, the industry monopolised by one system, and without any competition, will never make similar progress. Thus, the country will start declining in academic and industrial fields. Indeed, some industries can be, and should be, nationalised but wholesale nationalisation will sow the seeds of destruction of the country.

3. The above two will inevitably slow down the intellectual development and progress, and the human brain will ultimately be reduced to a machine.

4. Communism has also crushed individual sympathy and camaraderie inasmuch as the assistance of the poor and the deserving is in the hands of the government and no one else will have money to spare to help the poor or gift a dear one. As a result, the high moral values relating to love, friendship, sympathy, sacrifice, hospitality, helping the poor, kinship, and good-neighbourliness will start dying out and human society will become mechanised like everything else in the West.

5. Another drawback in communism is that it does not particularly prise higher intellectual capability, treating it on
a par with manual work. Such a system ultimately leads
to intellectual bankruptcy. This takes time. Therefore, all
these dangers are being ignored in the current enthusiasm.

In any case, communism is a natural reaction to a long-standing,
unjust system in Russia but the reaction took an extreme form.
As far as the nation is concerned, practically it means: out of the
frying pan of capitalism into the fire of communism.

Just Distribution of Wealth in Islam

By contrast, Islam, being a religion of nature and revealed by
the Creator of that nature, teaches moderation and the middle
course—avoiding both extremes. It does not deprive man of the
biggest natural incentive for individual effort; i.e. enjoying the
fruits of one's own labour. Neither does it pave the way for the
wealth to accumulate in a few hands or become the monopoly of
a particular section of the society. Islam has laid down very judicious basic rules, which are briefly outlined below:

First, Islam lays down a law of inheritance which, if adhered
to, leads to a fair distribution of wealth. According to Islamic law,
not only the eldest son or male children, but all children, sons and
daughters, also have the right to inherit. Moreover, the wife or
husband, mother and father, and sometimes sisters, brothers and
other close relatives, also share the inheritance. Consequently, the

wealth of the country is justly distributed and does not accumulate in a few hands.

Second, Islam forbids interest or usury. In addition to other ills associated with it, interest is a major cause of unjust distribution of wealth. By forbidding it, Islam has closed the door on accumulation of wealth in a few hands. Currently, because of the widespread use of interest, it may appear impossible to manage without it. But this is merely an illusion created by the current atmosphere. When Muslims ruled more than half the world, all trade was carried out without interest and so it shall be in future, God willing.

Third, Islam also declared gambling unlawful because that also opens the door for unjust distribution of wealth. It promotes waste of time and dependence on a lucky break instead of earning one's livelihood through dint of hard work, effort, and skill.

Fourth, Islam forbids hoarding of money; it should be invested in trade and industry to create jobs for the unemployed.

Fifth, Islam levies a heavy tax on the wealth of the rich in the form of Zakāt, to be distributed among the poor, the needy and the jobless who have a skill but lack the means to benefit from it. Islam has determined the purpose of the system of Zakāt as follows:

تُوْخَذُ مِنْ اَغْنِيَآءِهِمْ وَتُرَدُّ اِلٰى فُقَرَآءِهِمْ۔

Meaning: The proper use of Zakāt is to take a part from the wealth of rich people and distribute it among the poor and the needy. (*Ṣaḥīḥ al-Bukhārī, Kitābuz-Zakāt*)

Similarly, the mineral resources obtained, unearthed from private lands, are also levied a tax of 20% in order to help the poor.

Sixth, in addition to the compulsory tax of Zakāt, Islam has exhorted the Muslims to give alms to the poor, so that in addition to Zakāt administered by the government, people should also develop sympathy for their poor brothers and neighbours and that fosters the spirit of brotherhood, cooperation and camaraderie.

Seventh, if the above-mentioned measures fail to provide adequate assistance for all the poor, then it is binding on the government to help the needy from its own treasury so that everyone receives the basic necessities.

These are the seven principles whereby Islam has provided for the just distribution of wealth and assistance of the poor and the needy. (For a detailed study of Islam and Communism please refer to 'The Economic System of Islam' by Ḥaḍrat Khalifatul Masīḥ II and my treatise, 'Communism and Islam'). The fundamental concept is that an individual should be incentivised to make an effort and benefit from the success of his efforts, and his mental faculties should be honed through a sense of competition and achievement; at the same time, a just system of just distribution of wealth is applied by the state, and measures should be taken to continually reinvest the wealth of the nation for national interests. That is the wonderful middle course which staves off the ills of both sides (capitalism and communism) and incorporates the excellence of both, and that is the course adopted by Islam.

In short, as far as its basic principles are concerned, Russian communism is not directly related to atheism. It is merely an economic system which has indirectly attacked religion to strengthen itself. As already stated, it is a blind reaction that leads people from one extreme to the other and it carries the seed of its ultimate self-destruction. By contrast, Islam teaches moderation and justice. Certainly, when Russia wakes up, it will not find peace in anything but the natural religion of Islam.

CONCLUSION

Now I conclude this part of the discussion dealing with logical arguments for the existence of God. As I stated in the beginning, I want to reaffirm that I have avoided pedantic discussions and have elaborated on some simple points only. I have addressed myself mainly to the youth who, being immature, are sometimes influenced by modern teaching and adopt such views. What I have written, I reckon, should suffice a pure-hearted person and the remaining doubts can be resolved in the light of the principles that I have stated herein. As for those who are perverse, do not want to resolve their doubts, are blinkered by prejudice, and are unwilling to discern the truth, I have no remedy, nor does any one else except God. I pray that God may remove their doubts, grant them wisdom, and through His Grace, not let anyone pass away from this world without having recognised his Lord. Nothing would be more unfortunate for man than to leave this world without knowing the One who created him, sustained him and bestowed on him all his faculties.

I conclude with a beautiful excerpt from the writings of the Promised Messiah[as]:

How unfortunate is the person who still does not know that he has a God who has power over everything. Our paradise lies in our God, our highest delight is in our God, for we have seen Him and have found every beauty in Him. This wealth is worth procuring though one might have to lay down one's life to procure it; this ruby is worth purchasing though one may have to lose oneself to acquire it. O ye who are bereft! Run to this fountain, and it will satisfy you. It is the fountain of life that will save you. What shall I do and how shall I impress the hearts with this good news, and by beating what drum shall I make the announcement that this is your God, so that people might hear? What remedy shall I apply to the ears of the people so that they should listen? (*Kashtī-e-Nūḥ*)

EPILOGUE

By the Grace of God, I have now come to the end of the discussion on the logical arguments for the existence of God. As I mentioned in the beginning, these arguments can only lead man to the point where he realises that there ought to be a Creator and Master of this universe. But no matter how perfect and clear this belief may be, it is weaker and inferior to the belief that there is a God. The former is no more than a strong conjecture and a clear pointer, whereas the latter amounts to definite observation as if man has actually seen God and is left with no doubts and misgivings. The arguments for the latter kind of belief will be discussed, God willing, in the second part of the book. It will be shown how God, the Hidden and the One Beyond of Beyond, reveals Himself through the Prophets and *Auliyā'* and how these divines, through the miracles of His eternal knowledge and power, bring God close to the people's view as if He has descended on earth and is standing amidst His people. It is the same spectacle shown to the people by Ḥaḍrat Ādam^{as}, Ḥaḍrat Nūḥ^{as}, Ḥaḍrat Ibrāhīm^{as}, Ḥaḍrat Mūsā^{as}, Ḥaḍrat ʿĪsā^{as}, and Ḥaḍrat Muhammad^{saw}, during their times, respectively, and being shown by the Promised Messiah[as] during this age. In his capacity as the vicegerent of the Holy Prophet[saw], the Promised Messiah[as] thus speaks to the world:

> Come, and I will show you that God exists, and that He is All-Knowing. As a human being, I do not possess perfect knowledge, but when God tells me that such and such a thing will happen, although it is hidden behind a thousand veils, it happens exactly as God foretold. Come and test my claim. I will show you that God exists and He is the Almighty. As a human being I do not have perfect authority over anything, but God tells me He will do a particular thing in a particular way, and such work cannot be done by a human being in that manner and there are thousands of obstacles in the way, yet it happens the way He told me. Come and test my claim. I will show you that God exists, and that He is All-Hearing. He hears the prayers of His servants. I pray to God for things that are seemingly impossible, but because of my prayers He makes them happen. Come and test my claim. I will show you that God exists and He is the best Helper. When His pious servants are besieged from all sides with hardships and hostility, He opens ways of security for them. Come and test my claim. Come and let me show you that God exists, and that He is the Creator; being a human being, I do not have the power to create, but He manifests His creativity through me. He sprinkled the drops of His ink on my shirt without the aid of any material means. Come and test my claim. I will show you that God exists and He speaks. He speaks

with love and affection to His special people as He spoke
to me. Come and test my claim. I will show you that God
exists and He is the Lord of all the worlds, and nothing is
outside His providence. When He discontinues His providence for something, it cannot exist anymore, irrespective of what it is. Come and test my claim. I will show you
that God exists, and He is the Master, and none of His
creation can disobey Him. He can ordain whatever He
likes on whoever He likes. Come and let me show you His
manifestations in the sky. Come and let me show you His
manifestations in the earth. Come and let me show you
His manifestations in the air. Come and let me show you
His manifestations in water. Come and let me show you
His manifestations on the mountains. Come and let me
show you His manifestations on nations. Come and let
me show you His manifestations on rulers. Come and let
me show you His manifestations on hearts. Do come and
test my claim. (Taken from various books of the Promised
Messiah[as], Founder of the Ahmadiyya Movement)

A big claim, indeed! But think, if this claim is true, can atheism
survive? I swear by Him, in Whose hands is my life, and Whom I
will face after death, that the Promised Messiah[as] practically manifested all these signs (as I shall prove in the second part of the
book). The words of God revealed to the Promised Messiah[as] are
being fulfilled even today like the heavy rainfall from the sky, and
many will be fulfilled in the future. For instance, for the progress
of his God-given mission the Promised Messiah[as] states with great
authority:

O people! Listen, for this has been foretold by God who
created the earth and the heavens. He will spread this
Jamā'at of His in all countries, and will make them prevail
with the help of reason and arguments. The days are near,
nay they are at hand, when this shall be the only religion
looked upon with respect in the world. God will greatly
and wonderfully bless this faith and this movement,
and shall frustrate all those who will try to harm it. This
supremacy will continue until the Day of Judgement. [.]
I came only to sow the seed, so that seed has now been
sown by my hand and it will now grow and prosper and
there is none who can stop it. (*Tadhkiratush Shahādatain,*
pp. 64–65)

Then he says:

God has informed me again and again that He shall
give me great honour, and shall infuse my love in people's hearts. He shall spread my movement in the whole
world, and shall cause my sect to become dominant over
all others. People of my sect shall attain such perfection
in knowledge and learning that they will silence everyone with the light of their truthfulness, arguments and
signs. Every nation shall drink of this fountain, and this
movement shall spread fast until it shall dominate the
whole world. [.] God has addressed me with these words:
'I shall bless thee so much that kings shall seek blessings
from thy garments.' O ye who listen! Remember these
words and guard these prophecies. These are words of

God that will definitely be fulfilled one day. (*Tajalliyyāt-e-Ilāhiyyah*, p. 21)

With regard to the worldwide progress of Islam, for which he was ordained, the Promised Messiah[as] says:

Those days are near when the Sun of truth shall rise from the west and Europe shall learn about the True God. [...] The days are near when all religions but Islam shall perish. All stratagems shall come to naught but the heavenly stratagem of Islam that shall neither break nor become blunt, until it has smashed Dajjāliyat [Falsehood] into smithereens. The day comes when Divine Unity—which is felt even by those living in wilderness and those devoid of learning—shall spread in all countries. That day shall see the end of the false concept of atonement and no artificial god shall remain. With a single stroke, God shall do away with all the schemes of the disbelievers. But this shall come about neither by sword nor by the gun, but shall be wrought by bestowing light to ready spirits and by the descent of truth upon the hearts. Then only shall you understand what I tell you now. (*Tadhkirah*, pp. 285–286)

Does the present state of Ahmadiyya Jamāʻat, which is no better than a creeping ant in this vast world, and the present weakness of the Muslims, who are regarded as 'sick men', inspire hope of such a magnificent future? If not, and certainly not, and still it comes to pass as prophesied, will it not prove that there is an All-Knowing and All-Powerful God overseeing this world like a horseman holding the reins of the horse, guiding it along to a specified destination?

I now beg leave of my readers. Peace be upon those who accept the guidance sent by God.

وَاٰخِرُ دَعْوٰنَا اَنِ الْحَمْدُ لِلّٰهِ رَبِّ الْعٰلَمِيْنَ۔

[And our last prayer is that all praise belongs to Allah, the Master of the universe.]

A humble servant of the Lord of all the worlds,
Mirza Bashir Ahmad of Qadian

PUBLISHER'S NOTE

Please note that, in the translation that follows, words given in parentheses ( ) are the words of the Promised Messiah[as]. If any explanatory words or phrases are added by the translators for the purpose of clarification, they are put in square brackets [ ]. Footnotes given by the publisher are marked '[Publisher]'.

References to the Holy Quran contain the name of the *sūrah* [i.e. chapter] followed by a chapter:verse citation, e.g. *sūrah al-Jumu'ah*, 62:4, and counts *Bismillāhir-Raḥmānir-Raḥīm* [In the name of Allah, the Gracious, the Merciful] as the first verse in every chapter it appears.

The following abbreviations have been used; readers are urged to recite the full salutations when reading the book:

saw   *ṣallallāhu 'alaihi wa sallam*, meaning 'peace and blessings of Allah be upon him', is written after the name of the Holy Prophet Muhammad[saw].

as   *'alaihis-salām*, meaning 'peace be on him', is written after

the names of Prophets other than the Holy Prophet
Muhammad[saw].

ra   *radiyallāhu 'anhu/'anhā/'anhum*,   meaning 'Allah be
        pleased with him/her/them', is written after the names of
        the Companions of the Holy Prophet Muhammad[saw] or of
        the Promised Messiah[as].

rta   *rahmatullāh 'alaih/'alaihā/'alaihim*,   meaning 'Allah
        shower His mercy upon him/her/them', is written after
        the names of those deceased pious Muslims who are not
        Companions of the Holy Prophet Muhammad[saw] or of the
        Promised Messiah[as].

aba   *ayyadahullāhu Ta'ālā binasrihil-'Azīz*, meaning 'may Allah
        the Almighty help him with His powerful support', is written
        after the name of the present head of the Ahmadiyya Muslim
        Community, Hadrat Mirza Masroor Ahmad, Khalīfatul-
        Masīh V[aba].

In general, we have adopted the following system established by
the Royal Asiatic Society for our transliteration.

ا   at the beginning of a word, pronounced as *a, i, u* preceded
        by a very slight aspiration, like *h* in the English word
        honour.

ث   *th* – pronounced like *th* in the English word *thing*.

ح   *h* – a guttural aspirate, stronger than *h*.

خ   *kh* – pronounced like the Scottish *ch* in *loch*.

ذ   *dh* – pronounced like the English *th* in *that*.

ص   *ṣ* – strongly articulated *s*.

ض   *ḍ* – similar to the English *th* in *this*.

ط   *ṭ* – strongly articulated palatal *t*.

ظ   *ẓ* – strongly articulated *z*.

ع   ' – a strong guttural, the pronunciation of which must be learnt by the ear.

غ   *gh* – a sound similar to the French *r* in *grasseye,* and to the German *r*. It requires the muscles of the throat to be in the 'gargling' position to pronounce it.

ق   *q* – a deep guttural *k* sound.

ء   ' – a sort of catch in the voice.

Short vowels are represented by:

a   for ‾‾‾ (like *u* in *bud*).

i   for ‾‾‾ (like *i* in *bid*).

u   for ‾‾‾ (like *oo* in *wood*).

Long vowels by:

a   for ‾‾‾ or آ (like *a* in *father*).

i   for ى ‾‾‾ or ‾‾‾ (like *ee* in *deep*).

u   for و ‾‾‾ (like *oo* in *root*).

Other vowels by:

ai   for ى ‾‾‾ (like *i* in *site*).

au   for و ‾‾‾ (resembling *ou* in *sound*).

The consonants not included in the above list have the same phonetic value as in the principal languages of Europe. While the Arabic ن is represented by n, we have indicated the Urdu ں as ń. As noted above, the single quotation mark ʻ is used for transliterating ع which is distinct from the apostrophe ʼ used for ء.

We have not transliterated some Arabic words which have become part of English language, e.g. Islam, Quran, hadith, jihad, Ramadan, and ummah. The Royal Asiatic Society's rules of transliteration for names of persons, places, and other terms are not followed throughout the book as many of the names contain non-Arabic characters and carry a local transliteration and pronunciation style.

GLOSSARY

Aḥādīth *see* **Hadith**

Aḥmadiyya The Divinely appointed name for the Muslim Community established by the Prophet of the Latter Days. The root, Ahmad, is based on a proper name of the Holy Prophet^saw.

Āmīn A term which literally means, 'so be it' and is used at the end of a supplication to pray that God may accept it. It is similar in meaning to 'amen'.

Amīr Governor, president, or leader. Title for the national head of a chapter of the Ahmadiyya Muslim Community. (*also* Emir)

Anṣār Lit. 'Helpers'. Title accorded to the Muslims of Madinah who welcomed the Holy Prophet

Muhammad^saw upon his migration; *pl.* of Nāṣir.

Auliyā' A shorter version of *Auliyā'-ullāh*, which means, 'Friends of Allah'; *pl.* of Walī.

Ayyām *see* **Yaum**

Burūz Title applied to a person who is the spiritual reflection of an earlier holy personage and his qualities. The Promised Messiah^as was the reflection of the Holy Prophet^saw.

Dajjāl An Arabic word literally meaning the 'great deceiver'. In Islamic terminology, *dajjāl* refers to those satanic forces which would be unleashed in the Latter Days to oppose the Promised Messiah and Imām Mahdi^as.

Fiṭrah Human nature. The name given to those qualities invested in a child from its birth.

Hadith A saying of the Holy Prophet Muhammad^{saw}. The plural is *aḥādīth*.

Ḥaḍrat A term of respect used to show honour and reverence for a person of established righteousness and piety. Meaning include his/her Holiness, Worship, Eminence. It is also used for God in the superlative sense.

Jamā'at 'Community'. Refers here to the Ahmadiyya Muslim Community.

Khalīfah Caliph is derived from the Arabic word *khalīfah,* which means 'successor'. In Islamic terminology, the term righteous *khalīfah* is applied to each of the first four *khulafā'* who continued the mission of Ḥaḍrat Muhammad^{saw}, the Holy Prophet of Islam. Ahmadi Muslims refer to a successor of the Promised Messiah^{as} as Khalīfatul-Masīḥ. *pl. Khulafā'.*

Khalīfatul-Masīḥ *see* Khalīfah.

Khātamun-Nabiyyīn 'The Seal of the Prophets'. A title specific to the Holy Prohet Muhammad^{saw}, signifying his superiority to all his fellow Prophets.

Masīḥ 'Messiah'. Used here in reference to Ḥaḍrat 'Īsā [Jesus] Son or Mary.

Maulavī 'My master'. Used for Muslim religious clerics.

Muhājirīn 'Emigrants'. Refers to the people of Makkah who fled the city after more than ten years of persecution by the Quraish. *pl.* of Muhājir.

Mujaddid 'Reformer'. Each century after the Holy Prophet^{saw}, Allah raised a reformer(s) to revive the faith. The reformer of the 14th Islamic century was Ḥaḍrat Mirza Ghulam Ahmad^{as}.

Quraish The leading tribe in Makkah during the time of the Holy Prophet Muhammad^{saw}, who also belonged to the Quraish. They were also the most bitter in opposition to the Holy Prophet^{saw}.

Quran The final and perfect Scripture revealed by Allah for the guidance of mankind for all times to come. It was revealed word-by-word to the Holy Prophet Muhammad^{saw} over a period of twenty-three years.

Sūfī A practitioner of *taṣawwaf* [i.e. Sufism], concerned with the inner, mystical dimension of Islam.

Ṣulaḥā' Plural of Ṣāliḥ which means good, just, and honest person or action. The term Ṣulaḥā' is used in Islamic termonology to denote the first grade of righteousness. The higher grades are the Shuahadā' (martyrs) Ṣiddiquīn (the truthful) and Nabiyyīn (the prophets).

Sūrah A chapter of the Holy Quran.

Yaum Day, age, epoch.

Zakāt 'That which purifies'. One of the five pillars of Islam; also referred to as almsgiving.

Ẓill Title applied to a person who is the spiritual shadow of an earlier holy personage, following in their footsteps. The Promised Messiah[as] was the spiritual shadow of the Holy Prophet[saw].

INDEX